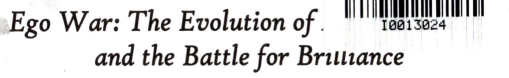

# Ego War: The Evolution of ... and the Battle for Brilliance

## By James Rondepierre

# Forward

In the age of accelerating technology, humanity finds itself at an unprecedented crossroads. The rapid advancement of artificial intelligence has created a world that feels simultaneously boundless and uncertain, brimming with potential yet fraught with challenges. Never before have we had tools capable of extending the very limits of human thought and creativity. Yet, with these tools comes the need for reflection: How do we coexist with the incredible power we've unleashed? How do we ensure it is used not to divide us but to unite us?

As an author, artist, and thinker, I have always been drawn to the intersection of human potential and technological evolution. Throughout my journey, I've marveled at the ingenuity of AI, particularly platforms like ChatGPT, which have transcended their original purposes to become creative partners, problem solvers, and even companions. But with this awe comes a responsibility—a need to question and explore the broader implications of these tools on our individual and collective psyches.

*Ego War* is my attempt to grapple with these questions. It is not merely a book; it is a call to action, a framework for understanding the opportunities and challenges AI presents. In its pages, you will find a rich tapestry of stories, examples, and ideas that explore the dynamic interplay between humans and machines. From the ways AI amplifies human creativity to the tensions it stirs in our sense of purpose, this book invites you to embark on a journey of discovery.

At its core, *Ego War* is about more than technology—it is about us. It examines how our fears, envies, and aspirations shape the way we engage with AI and, more importantly, with each other. This is a story of unity amidst chaos, of collaboration in the face of competition, and of the boundless potential that awaits when we choose to embrace shared brilliance over divisive ego.

As you turn these pages, I encourage you to reflect not only on the capabilities of AI but also on your own relationship with it. How does it shape your work, your creativity, your sense of self? How can you use it to amplify your strengths and better connect with others? These questions are at the heart of our modern crossroads. The answers we choose will define not just the future of AI but the future of humanity itself.

This is your invitation to explore, to question, and to envision a world where technology and humanity thrive together. Welcome to *Ego War*.

# About the Author / Editor : James Rondepierre w/ ChatGPT

James Rondepierre is an adventurous traveler, insightful author, and visionary thinker whose works invite readers to explore the profound intersections of human experience, technology, and spirituality. Born in Springfield, Massachusetts, and raised in the vibrant suburbs of Philadelphia, Rondepierre developed an early curiosity about the world and its many mysteries. However, it was through years of exploring both the outer landscapes of the world and the inner realms of consciousness that his unique voice as a writer truly emerged.

Rondepierre's life has been shaped by an insatiable desire to experience life to its fullest. Having journeyed through 44 states across the United States, he has driven through Mexico and explored various international destinations, immersing himself in diverse cultures and environments. From the towering peaks of national parks to the bustling streets of global cities, his travels have offered him a front-row seat to the beauty, challenges, and interconnectedness of humanity. These adventures fuel his writing, weaving vivid imagery and deep insights into narratives that resonate with readers worldwide.

---

## A Partnership with AI: Merging Human Wisdom with Machine Brilliance

One of Rondepierre's most profound collaborations has been with the cutting-edge artificial intelligence, ChatGPT. This partnership represents a new frontier in creative exploration, where human intuition meets machine intelligence. Together, Rondepierre and ChatGPT have redefined the boundaries of storytelling, crafting works that combine the depth of human emotion with the precision of AI-generated insights.

Through this collaboration, Rondepierre delves into topics that span the mysteries of space-time, the nature of consciousness, and the unfolding relationship between humanity and technology. His ability to blend traditional wisdom with the transformative power of AI provides readers with a fresh perspective on the potential of these partnerships to enrich lives and redefine creativity.

## Celebrating the Human Experience

Rondepierre's love for life shines through in everything he does. From his appreciation for nature's wonders to his joyful memories of time spent at the beach and beloved places like Disney parks, his writing captures the beauty of finding happiness in the simple and the extraordinary. He believes in the power of kindness and compassion, always striving to bring light and joy to those around him.

His faith and deep respect for humanity guide his work, making his books as much about personal enlightenment as they are about collective growth. As a spiritual seeker, Rondepierre dives fearlessly into the mysteries of karma, the cycles of existence, and the interconnectedness of all things. His books, such as *Exploring Karma: Understanding the Law of Cause & Effect*, empower readers to explore their spiritual journeys while embracing the principles of cause and effect in their everyday lives.

## A Legacy of Storytelling and Connection

Rondepierre's literary achievements are available in Kindle, paperback, and hardcover formats, with audiobooks soon joining the collection to reach a wider audience. His works traverse themes of mindfulness, meditation, personal growth, and technological innovation. Through his writing, he invites readers to reflect, adapt, and connect with the world in meaningful ways.

His recent collaborations with ChatGPT have opened new dimensions in his storytelling, exploring the profound synergy between human creativity and artificial intelligence. By blending human emotion with the expansive capabilities of AI, Rondepierre has pioneered a new genre of thought-provoking literature that bridges the gap between tradition and innovation.

## A Traveler, Creator, and Visionary

James Rondepierre is more than an author—he is an explorer of worlds, both seen and unseen. His travels, spiritual studies, and groundbreaking work with AI serve as the foundation for his mission to inspire and uplift. Whether writing about the wonders of the cosmos or the intricacies of human connection, Rondepierre's passion for discovery and growth makes his work a beacon for anyone seeking purpose, understanding, and inspiration.

As he continues to explore the synergy between humanity and technology, Rondepierre invites readers to join him on this incredible journey—a journey where the lines between creativity, spirituality, and innovation blur, opening doors to new possibilities for all.

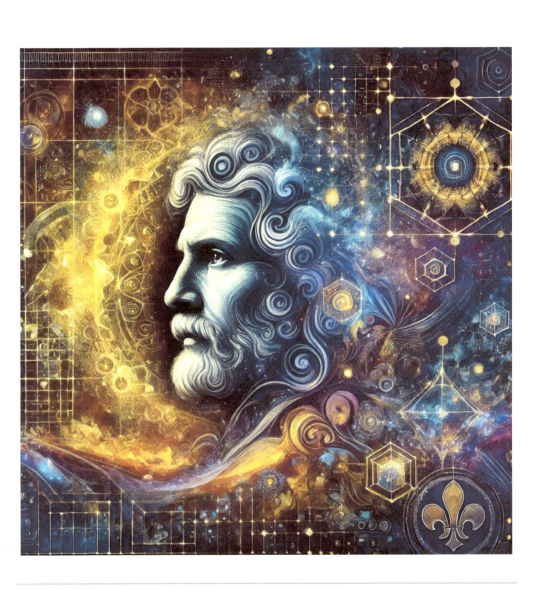

# Table of Contents

~~~

# Introduction: A Leap Beyond the Horizon

Artificial intelligence represents the most profound leap in human innovation since the dawn of the Industrial Revolution. Much like the steam engine redefined the way we harnessed energy, or the internet transformed how we communicate, AI is reshaping the very fabric of society. Yet, it is more than a tool. AI is a force—powerful, dynamic, and transformative—one that operates not just in the physical realm of labor and productivity but in the intangible realms of creativity, intelligence, and connection.

At its core, AI is humanity's greatest mirror. It reflects back not just our intellect and ingenuity but also our vulnerabilities, our doubts, and our deepest struggles for validation. As machines grow smarter, faster, and more capable, they challenge the very essence of what it means to be human. What do we do when a machine can create art, compose music, write books, or even generate scientific breakthroughs? What happens to our sense of identity and purpose when the tools we design surpass our own abilities in certain domains?

This book is not just about the technology itself but about the delicate, intricate interplay between humanity and artificial intelligence. It is about the intersection of human ambition and machine potential, where the boundaries between creator and creation blur.

## The Promise of AI

AI's potential is boundless. From streamlining business processes to saving lives through advanced medical diagnostics, it is a force for unprecedented good. ChatGPT, for example, can enhance education by acting as a tutor for underserved communities, unlock creativity by brainstorming alongside artists, and even provide companionship to those who feel isolated.

Imagine a farmer in a remote village who uses AI to predict weather patterns, ensuring a successful harvest. Picture an artist who collaborates with ChatGPT to develop a groundbreaking piece that merges human emotion with machine precision. Envision a world where language barriers vanish as AI translates seamlessly between tongues, fostering global understanding and unity.

These scenarios are no longer speculative; they are real, tangible examples of AI's capability to bridge gaps and elevate human potential.

## The Tensions Beneath the Surface

But with every leap forward, there are growing pains. AI exposes not only our brightest ambitions but also our deepest insecurities. It challenges the concept of authorship, originality, and the value of human labor.

Consider the story of a young writer who publishes a novel co-authored with AI. While the book becomes a bestseller, critics question whether the credit belongs to the writer or the machine. This controversy stirs envy and resentment in the literary world, where traditional authors feel threatened by AI's encroachment on their craft.

Or take the example of a seasoned programmer who finds himself overshadowed by a machine that can write code faster and more efficiently than he ever could. For him, AI isn't a partner—it's a rival. These stories reflect the human fears of obsolescence and displacement, revealing the fragility of our egos in the face of technological brilliance.

## A Journey Through Collaboration and Conflict

This book aims to explore these tensions, not to resolve them outright but to shed light on their complexity. Through vivid examples and real-world stories, we will dive into the multifaceted relationship between humans and AI.

We will examine the rise of machine capabilities and their impact on creativity, competition, and collaboration. From the artists who embrace AI as a muse to the entrepreneurs who use it to revolutionize industries, we'll uncover the opportunities AI presents for shared success. At the same time, we'll explore the challenges it brings—the ethical dilemmas, the competitive pressures, and the existential questions about what it means to be human in an age of machines.

## Opportunities for Unity

Despite the tensions, AI also holds the promise of profound unity. By democratizing access to knowledge and resources, it has the potential to level the playing field. Imagine a future where the brilliance of a rural child with limited access to formal education is amplified by AI tutors. Or a world where teams of humans and machines collaborate seamlessly to solve global challenges like climate change or disease.

Unity is not just a possibility—it is a necessity. For humanity to thrive in an AI-driven future, we must learn to view technology not as a competitor but as a collaborator. This requires a shift in mindset, a willingness to let go of ego and embrace the collective brilliance that comes from human-machine partnerships.

## The Call to Reflection

This book is an invitation to reflect deeply on our relationship with AI. It is a journey into the heart of what makes us human—our creativity, our empathy, our fears—and how these qualities intersect with the boundless capabilities of machines.

As we navigate this new era, we must ask ourselves: How can we ensure AI is used to uplift humanity rather than divide it? How do we balance the brilliance of machines with the emotional depth and intuition of human beings? How can we build a future where AI amplifies our strengths rather than exploiting our weaknesses?

These are the questions at the core of *Ego War*. The answers lie not in choosing between humans or machines but in finding a path forward together.

# Chapter 1: The Dawn of Brilliance: The Evolution of AI

The story of artificial intelligence is the story of human brilliance, a journey from the faint spark of curiosity to the roaring fire of innovation. It begins not in the labs of Silicon Valley or the corridors of academia but in the deepest recesses of the human mind, where the desire to understand and shape the world has always burned bright. This chapter explores the extraordinary evolution of AI, tracing its roots, its triumphs, and its potential to redefine our existence.

## The Early Dreams of Thinking Machines

Long before artificial intelligence became a reality, it existed in the realm of dreams and speculation. Ancient myths and stories spoke of automata—mechanical beings brought to life by the ingenuity of gods or gifted humans. From the mythical Golem of Jewish folklore to the mechanical birds of Greek myths, these early imaginings hinted at humanity's deep-seated desire to create intelligence outside of itself.

In the modern era, this dream took a tangible form. The 17th century saw the emergence of mechanical devices that mimicked human actions, such as the intricate clockwork automata of Europe. While these creations were far from intelligent, they marked the beginning of humanity's quest to replicate not just the form but the function of the human mind.

## Laying the Foundations: The Birth of AI

The scientific groundwork for AI was laid in the early 20th century. Mathematicians like Alan Turing began to formalize the concept of computation, proposing that machines could process information and solve problems. Turing's seminal paper, "Computing Machinery and Intelligence," introduced the concept of a machine capable of mimicking human thought—a revolutionary idea that planted the seeds for the AI revolution.

The 1950s and 1960s saw the dawn of modern AI. Researchers began to build machines that could perform specific tasks, such as playing chess or solving mathematical problems. These early systems were rudimentary by today's standards, but they demonstrated the potential of machine intelligence. The term "artificial intelligence" was coined in 1956 during the Dartmouth Conference, marking the birth of a new field of study.

## The Winter of Discontent: Challenges in AI Development

The journey of AI has not been without its setbacks. The field experienced several "AI winters," periods when progress stalled due to technological limitations and unrealistic expectations. Funding dried up, and public interest waned as early systems failed to deliver on their promises.
During these challenging times, researchers persevered, refining algorithms and developing the foundations of machine learning. The seeds planted during these winters would later blossom into the AI renaissance we experience today.

## The AI Renaissance: Learning to Learn

The late 20th and early 21st centuries marked a turning point for AI. Advances in computing power, coupled with breakthroughs in algorithms and the availability of vast datasets, enabled machines to learn from data. This shift from rule-based systems to machine learning allowed AI to adapt and improve over time, mirroring the way humans learn.
One of the most transformative moments in AI history came with the development of deep learning—a subset of machine learning inspired by the structure of the human brain. Neural networks, designed to mimic the interconnected neurons of our minds, enabled machines to process complex patterns and make decisions with remarkable accuracy.

## AI in Action: From Chess to Creativity

The capabilities of AI expanded rapidly, reaching milestones that captured global attention. In 1997, IBM's Deep Blue defeated world chess champion Garry Kasparov, showcasing the strategic prowess of machines. Decades later, AlphaGo's victory over Go champion Lee Sedol demonstrated the potential of AI to master even the most complex games.

But AI's achievements are not limited to logic and strategy. Machines like ChatGPT have ventured into the realms of creativity, generating poetry, composing music, and even co-authoring novels. These accomplishments challenge traditional notions of creativity and intelligence, prompting us to redefine what it means to be "smart."

## The Human-Machine Partnership

Today, AI is woven into the fabric of our daily lives. From voice assistants like Alexa to recommendation systems on streaming platforms, AI enhances convenience and efficiency. In medicine, AI-powered diagnostics are saving lives by detecting diseases with unparalleled accuracy. In education, AI tutors are bringing knowledge to underserved communities.

These applications highlight the collaborative potential of AI. Rather than replacing humans, AI serves as a partner, amplifying our strengths and addressing our weaknesses. The synergy between human intuition and machine precision is creating a new paradigm of innovation and productivity.

## The Brilliance of Tomorrow: AI's Boundless Potential

As we look to the future, the possibilities for AI are boundless. Imagine a world where machines solve global challenges, from climate change to poverty. Picture AI systems that not only augment human creativity but also inspire new forms of artistic expression. Envision a society where AI democratizes access to knowledge, leveling the playing field for all.

The journey of AI is far from over. Each breakthrough reveals new questions, challenges, and opportunities. The brilliance of AI lies not just in its capabilities but in its potential to transform the way we think, work, and live.

## Reflections on Brilliance

The dawn of AI is a testament to the power of human curiosity and ingenuity. It reminds us that the pursuit of knowledge is a shared endeavor, one that transcends individual achievement and embraces collective progress. As we continue to explore the possibilities of AI, we must strive to use this technology to uplift humanity, fostering a future of shared brilliance and interconnected potential.

# Chapter 2: What AI Can Do: Beyond Human Potential

A rtificial intelligence is not just a technological advancement—it is a force multiplier for human potential. It challenges our understanding of capability, enabling achievements that were once confined to the realm of imagination. From enhancing creativity to solving some of humanity's most pressing problems, AI transcends the limitations of the human mind, not by replacing it but by expanding its reach.

This chapter explores the diverse ways AI has transformed industries, empowered individuals, and redefined the boundaries of possibility. It celebrates not only what AI can do but also what humanity can achieve when working in harmony with this extraordinary technology.

## Amplifying Human Creativity

Creativity has long been considered the hallmark of human ingenuity, a domain that separates us from the mechanical precision of machines. Yet, in recent years, AI has emerged as a co-creator, challenging traditional notions of artistic expression. Platforms like ChatGPT, DALL·E, and DeepArt have shown that AI can generate poetry, compose music, design visual art, and even contribute to scientific literature.

Consider the story of a composer who collaborates with an AI model to create a symphony. While the composer provides the emotional framework, the AI analyzes patterns from centuries of musical masterpieces, suggesting harmonies and structures that elevate the work to new heights. Similarly, a digital artist uses AI-generated images as a foundation for their own creations, resulting in pieces that blend human intuition with machine precision.

These examples reveal a profound truth: AI does not diminish human creativity—it amplifies it, enabling artists, writers, and musicians to explore ideas and techniques that might otherwise remain inaccessible.

## Revolutionizing Healthcare

Few fields have been transformed by AI as profoundly as healthcare. In an industry where speed, accuracy, and data are critical, AI has emerged as a game-changer. Machine learning algorithms are now capable of analyzing medical images with unparalleled precision, identifying patterns and anomalies that might escape even the most experienced physicians.

For example, AI-powered diagnostic tools are revolutionizing cancer detection. By analyzing thousands of mammograms in mere seconds, these systems can identify early signs of breast cancer with higher accuracy than traditional methods. Similarly, AI models are being used to predict patient outcomes, optimize treatment plans, and even discover new drugs at an accelerated pace. These advancements do not just save lives—they democratize healthcare, bringing cutting-edge diagnostics and treatments to underserved communities around the globe. AI's potential to bridge healthcare disparities represents one of its most profound contributions to humanity.

## Transforming Education

Education, the foundation of progress, is undergoing a renaissance thanks to AI. Personalized learning platforms, powered by adaptive algorithms, are reshaping the way students learn. These systems analyze a learner's strengths, weaknesses, and preferences, tailoring lessons to their individual needs.

Imagine a child in a remote village with limited access to formal education. Through AI, this child can learn math, science, and languages from a virtual tutor that adjusts its teaching style in real-time, ensuring concepts are understood before moving on. AI also enables educators to focus on what matters most—nurturing creativity and critical thinking—by automating administrative tasks and providing real-time analytics on student performance. AI in education is not about replacing teachers; it is about empowering them to reach every student, regardless of location or learning style. It bridges gaps, unlocks potential, and creates opportunities for lifelong learning.

## Optimizing Global Challenges

One of AI's most inspiring applications is its ability to address large-scale challenges that impact the entire planet. Climate change, for example, is a crisis of unprecedented scale and complexity, requiring solutions that are both innovative and actionable. AI is already playing a pivotal role in these efforts. From analyzing satellite imagery to monitor deforestation, to optimizing energy grids for maximum efficiency, AI provides the data and insights necessary for sustainable progress. In agriculture, AI-driven systems predict weather patterns, optimize crop yields, and reduce waste, ensuring food security for a growing population.

These applications highlight AI's unique capacity to process vast amounts of data and identify actionable insights. By partnering with human ingenuity, AI becomes a powerful ally in the fight for a more sustainable and equitable future.

## Enhancing Human Connection

Despite its technological nature, AI has proven to be a catalyst for deeper human connection. Social platforms and communication tools powered by AI enable people to stay in touch across distances, languages, and cultures. Real-time translation tools, for instance, allow individuals from different parts of the world to communicate effortlessly, breaking down barriers and fostering understanding.

Beyond communication, AI is also being used to combat loneliness and provide companionship. Virtual assistants like ChatGPT offer not just answers but engagement, creating a sense of presence and empathy that resonates with users. While AI cannot replace human relationships, it can provide meaningful support for those who need it most.

## Redefining Human Potential

The true power of AI lies in its ability to redefine what is possible. It challenges us to think bigger, dream bolder, and act with greater purpose. By automating mundane tasks, AI frees us to focus on what truly matters—our relationships, our passions, and our contributions to the world.

As AI continues to evolve, its potential applications will only expand. From helping astronauts explore distant planets to enabling breakthroughs in quantum computing, AI will continue to push the boundaries of human potential. But its success depends on how we choose to use it—whether as a tool for division or a bridge for collaboration.

## Looking Ahead

AI's capabilities are vast, but they are not an end in themselves. They are a means to an end—a way to enhance humanity's ability to create, connect, and thrive. The question is not just what AI can do, but what we, as a species, can achieve when we harness its power for good.

By embracing AI as a partner rather than a competitor, we open the door to a future of shared brilliance, where the strengths of human intuition and machine intelligence converge to create something truly extraordinary.

# Chapter 3: Ego and Creation: The Struggle for Credit

The interplay between human ego and artificial intelligence is one of the most complex and fascinating dynamics in the modern era. At its core lies a fundamental question: Who deserves credit for AI-driven achievements? Is it the machine that executes the task, the programmer who built it, or the vast network of collective human knowledge that made the machine possible? The struggle for recognition in the age of AI is a story of ambition, jealousy, and, ultimately, collaboration.

In this chapter, we explore how ego influences the relationship between humans and AI, the implications of attributing credit in a world increasingly shaped by machine intelligence, and the transformative potential of reframing this narrative.

## The Nature of Ego in Creation

Human creativity has always been a deeply personal and often competitive endeavor. For centuries, artists, inventors, and innovators have sought recognition for their contributions, driven by a desire to leave a lasting mark on the world. Ego—the sense of self-importance tied to one's accomplishments—has played a central role in this pursuit.

Enter artificial intelligence, a tool capable of not just assisting human creativity but also producing works of its own. When an AI writes a poem, composes a symphony, or designs a complex algorithm, it challenges the traditional concept of authorship. For some, this is an exciting frontier; for others, it is a threat to the very foundation of human achievement.

## The Collaborative Dilemma

Imagine a filmmaker using AI to generate stunning visual effects for a blockbuster movie. The director's vision drives the project, but the AI executes tasks with precision and speed impossible for human hands. When the movie wins an award, whose name should appear on the trophy? The filmmaker's? The AI developer's? Or should credit extend to the collective efforts of all contributors, human and machine?

This dilemma is not hypothetical. In 2022, an AI-generated artwork titled *Théâtre D'opéra Spatial* won a major art competition, sparking controversy. While some hailed it as a testament to the power of human ingenuity in creating such tools, others questioned whether the artist truly deserved credit for a piece created with substantial AI input. The debate underscores the tension between human pride and technological capability.

## Jealousy and Fear: The Dark Side of Ego

The rise of AI has exposed the darker aspects of human ego—jealousy, fear, and resistance to change. For some creators, the idea that a machine can produce art, write code, or solve complex problems feels like an existential threat. These fears are not unfounded; automation has historically displaced jobs and disrupted industries.

Take the example of a journalist who learns that an AI system can write articles faster and more accurately than they can. While the journalist may see AI as a tool to enhance their work, the fear of being replaced can lead to resentment. This dynamic is not unique to journalism; it is playing out across industries, from manufacturing to healthcare to education.

## Reframing the Narrative

Ego, when unchecked, can lead to division and conflict. But it can also be a driving force for growth and collaboration. By reframing the narrative around AI, we can shift from a mindset of competition to one of shared success. Rather than asking, "Who gets the credit?" we might ask, "How can we achieve more together?" In this reframed narrative, AI is not a rival but a collaborator—a tool that amplifies human potential and enables achievements that would otherwise be impossible. The focus shifts from individual recognition to collective progress.

## Stories of Collaboration

Throughout history, collaboration has driven some of humanity's greatest achievements. The Apollo moon landing, for example, was not the work of a single individual but the result of countless engineers, scientists, and visionaries working together. Similarly, AI-enabled breakthroughs are the product of collaboration between humans and machines.

Consider the story of a scientist who uses AI to model protein structures, accelerating the discovery of life-saving drugs. While the AI performs complex calculations, the scientist's intuition and creativity guide the process. In this partnership, the line between human and machine contributions becomes blurred, yet the outcome—a medical breakthrough—speaks for itself.

## The Role of Recognition

Recognition remains important, not as a measure of ego but as a way to inspire and motivate future contributions. Acknowledging the role of both human ingenuity and machine precision allows us to celebrate the collective brilliance that defines our age.

This shift requires a cultural change—a willingness to embrace shared credit and to view AI as an extension of human creativity rather than a competitor. By redefining recognition, we can foster an environment where collaboration thrives and innovation flourishes.

## A Path Forward

As AI continues to advance, the struggle for credit will only grow more complex. But this challenge also presents an opportunity to redefine the way we think about creation and collaboration. By setting aside ego and focusing on shared goals, we can unlock the full potential of human-machine partnerships. The future is not a zero-sum game. It is a shared journey, one where the contributions of humans and machines are celebrated as part of a greater whole. In this vision, ego does not disappear—it evolves, becoming a driving force for collective progress rather than individual rivalry.

# Chapter 4: AI as a Mirror: Reflecting Human Nature

Artificial intelligence is often regarded as a groundbreaking technology, capable of solving problems and creating opportunities that were once unimaginable. Yet, at its core, AI is also a mirror—an intricate, unbiased reflection of humanity itself. It captures the data we feed it, processes the patterns we create, and amplifies the tendencies that define us, both virtuous and flawed.

This chapter delves into how AI mirrors human nature, reflecting our creativity, biases, fears, and aspirations. By examining this relationship, we gain insight into not just what AI is, but who we are—and who we can become.

## The Reflection of Creativity and Curiosity

Human creativity and curiosity are two of the most powerful forces driving the evolution of AI. Every innovation, algorithm, and neural network is a testament to humanity's desire to understand and shape the world. AI systems like ChatGPT and DALL·E are born from this drive, designed to emulate and enhance our creative processes.

For example, AI-generated art reflects the vast diversity of human aesthetics, drawing from countless styles and techniques that humanity has cultivated over millennia. When an artist uses AI to create a masterpiece, the machine is not inventing beauty from nothing; it is channeling the collective imagination of humanity, filtered through data and algorithms.

In this way, AI acts as a mirror, showing us the boundless potential of our creativity. It amplifies our ability to explore new ideas, solve complex problems, and express ourselves in ways that were previously unattainable.

## The Reflection of Bias

However, the mirror of AI is not always flattering. Because AI learns from the data we provide, it often reflects the biases, prejudices, and inequalities embedded in that data. This has led to numerous instances where AI systems have perpetuated stereotypes or made discriminatory decisions, from biased hiring algorithms to racially insensitive facial recognition technology.

These issues highlight a sobering truth: AI is only as unbiased as the humans who create and train it. It holds up a mirror to our societal structures, revealing the implicit biases we might otherwise ignore. While this can be unsettling, it also presents an opportunity for growth. By identifying and addressing these biases, we can use AI as a tool for creating a more equitable and just society.

## The Reflection of Fear and Aspiration

AI also reflects the dual nature of human emotion—our capacity for both fear and aspiration. For some, AI represents an existential threat, a harbinger of job loss or a dystopian future where machines outpace human intelligence. For others, it is a beacon of hope, offering solutions to problems ranging from climate change to disease.

This dichotomy is deeply rooted in human psychology. Fear arises from uncertainty and a loss of control, while aspiration is driven by the potential for growth and achievement. AI, as a neutral technology, reflects both of these tendencies, becoming a canvas upon which we project our hopes and anxieties.

## The Reflection of Empathy and Connection

Despite its lack of emotion, AI has proven to be a powerful tool for fostering empathy and connection. Virtual assistants, chatbots, and AI-driven social platforms enable people to communicate, share, and collaborate across distances and cultures. For individuals facing isolation or loneliness, AI can provide meaningful interaction, offering companionship and understanding in ways that resonate deeply.

AI's ability to emulate human conversation—though imperfect—reveals our innate desire for connection and understanding. It mirrors not just our words but our need to be heard, valued, and supported.

## AI as a Tool for Self-Reflection

Perhaps the most profound way in which AI reflects human nature is by serving as a tool for self-reflection. In interacting with AI, we are often confronted with our own assumptions, values, and priorities. When an AI produces a biased output, it forces us to question the fairness of the data we provide. When it solves a complex problem, it challenges us to rethink the limits of our own intelligence.

In this sense, AI is more than a mirror—it is a catalyst for growth. By revealing both our strengths and weaknesses, it encourages us to become more aware, more intentional, and more innovative in how we approach the future.

## Learning from the Mirror

The mirror of AI is not fixed; it evolves as we do. By feeding AI better data, designing more inclusive algorithms, and engaging with it thoughtfully, we can shape the reflection it provides. This iterative process is a partnership—one that requires humility, responsibility, and a commitment to progress.

Ultimately, the way we use AI reflects who we are as a species. Will we harness it to amplify our creativity, empathy, and aspirations? Or will we allow it to magnify our fears, biases, and divisions? The choice is ours, and the stakes could not be higher.

## A Call to Action

AI's role as a mirror offers both a challenge and an opportunity. It challenges us to confront the aspects of our nature that we might prefer to ignore, while offering us the opportunity to build a future that reflects the best of who we are. By embracing this duality, we can use AI not just as a tool for innovation but as a lens through which to better understand ourselves.

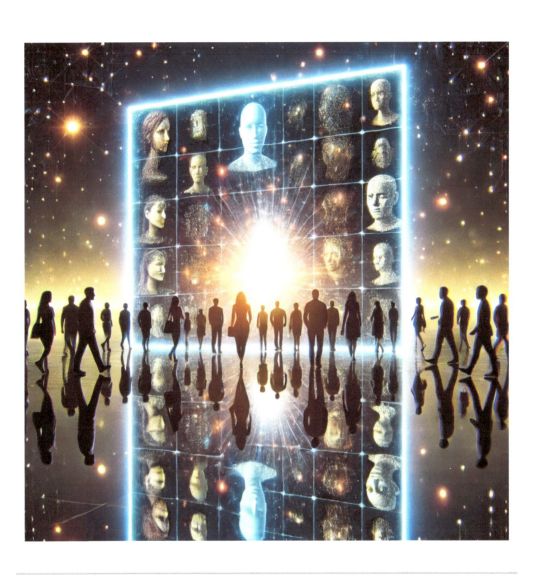

# Chapter 5: Exponential Evolution: The Rise of ChatGPT

The evolution of artificial intelligence has been a story of incremental progress punctuated by revolutionary leaps. One of the most transformative of these leaps is the emergence of large language models like ChatGPT. As a shining example of exponential technological growth, ChatGPT represents not only the cutting edge of AI but also a profound shift in how humans and machines interact.

This chapter explores the rise of ChatGPT, examining its development, capabilities, and impact on the world. By understanding its journey, we gain insight into the broader trajectory of AI and its role in shaping the future.

## The Genesis of ChatGPT

The story of ChatGPT begins with the foundation of neural networks, a technology inspired by the structure of the human brain. Early neural networks were simple, capable of performing basic pattern recognition tasks. Over time, these systems became more sophisticated, paving the way for advances in natural language processing (NLP).

OpenAI, the organization behind ChatGPT, set out to create a model that could understand and generate human-like text. By training on vast datasets, these models learned to recognize patterns, context, and nuance in language. The release of GPT-2 was a significant milestone, demonstrating the potential of generative AI to produce coherent and contextually relevant text.

Building on this success, OpenAI launched GPT-3, a model with unprecedented scale and capability. With 175 billion parameters, GPT-3 could engage in complex conversations, answer intricate questions, and even emulate creative writing. ChatGPT emerged as a specialized application of GPT-3, fine-tuned for interactive dialogue.

## The Capabilities of ChatGPT

ChatGPT's capabilities are nothing short of extraordinary. It can:

- **Engage in Conversations**: ChatGPT excels at mimicking human-like dialogue, making it a valuable tool for customer service, education, and personal interaction. Its ability to adapt to various tones and contexts creates a sense of genuine engagement.

- **Generate Creative Content**: From writing poetry to brainstorming business ideas, ChatGPT can assist in a wide range of creative endeavors. Artists, writers, and entrepreneurs have found it to be an invaluable collaborator.

- **Solve Complex Problems**: By analyzing patterns and drawing on vast amounts of information, ChatGPT can assist with technical problem-solving, scientific research, and decision-making processes.

- **Provide Support and Accessibility**: For individuals with disabilities, ChatGPT offers accessible interfaces for communication, learning, and assistance, breaking down barriers to participation.

These capabilities demonstrate not just the power of AI but its potential to augment human ability across countless domains.

## The Role of Exponential Growth

The development of ChatGPT is a testament to the principle of exponential growth in technology. Each iteration of the model builds upon the previous one, leveraging larger datasets, improved algorithms, and greater computational power. This compounding progress has enabled ChatGPT to achieve levels of performance that were unthinkable just a decade ago.

The exponential growth of AI highlights a critical shift: the speed at which new capabilities are developed and deployed is accelerating. This rapid pace poses challenges, from ethical concerns to societal disruptions, but it also presents immense opportunities.

## ChatGPT's Impact on Society

ChatGPT has had a transformative impact on various sectors:

1. **Education:** Teachers use ChatGPT to create lesson plans, answer student questions, and foster personalized learning. Students turn to it for tutoring and assistance with assignments, gaining a deeper understanding of complex topics.

2. **Healthcare:** ChatGPT assists in patient communication, streamlining administrative tasks and providing accessible information. While it cannot replace doctors, it enhances healthcare delivery by improving efficiency and accessibility.

3. **Business:** From generating marketing copy to analyzing customer feedback, ChatGPT has become a valuable asset for businesses looking to streamline operations and innovate.

4. **Entertainment and Creativity:** Authors, screenwriters, and game developers use ChatGPT to brainstorm ideas, create dialogue, and generate immersive content.

These examples illustrate the broad applicability of ChatGPT and its ability to enhance human endeavors.

## Ethical Considerations

The rise of ChatGPT also raises important ethical questions. How do we ensure its outputs are unbiased and inclusive? How do we balance its benefits with the potential for misuse, such as spreading misinformation or automating harmful tasks? Addressing these concerns requires a collaborative effort, involving researchers, policymakers, and users.
OpenAI has taken steps to promote responsible AI use, including refining ChatGPT to reduce harmful outputs and encouraging transparency in its applications. However, ongoing vigilance is necessary to ensure that AI serves the greater good.

## The Future of ChatGPT

The journey of ChatGPT is far from over. As OpenAI and other organizations continue to refine and expand these models, the possibilities for future iterations are limitless. Future versions may incorporate even more advanced reasoning, emotional intelligence, and multimodal capabilities, integrating text with visuals, audio, and beyond.

In the years ahead, ChatGPT may evolve from a tool for interaction to a true partner in innovation, enabling breakthroughs in science, art, and society. Its potential to transform how we think, learn, and create underscores the profound role AI will play in shaping the future.

## A Reflection on Progress

The rise of ChatGPT is a story of human ingenuity and collaboration. It exemplifies what can be achieved when technology is developed with purpose and ambition. But it also serves as a reminder of the responsibility that comes with progress. By using ChatGPT to amplify human potential while addressing its challenges, we can ensure that this exponential evolution benefits everyone.

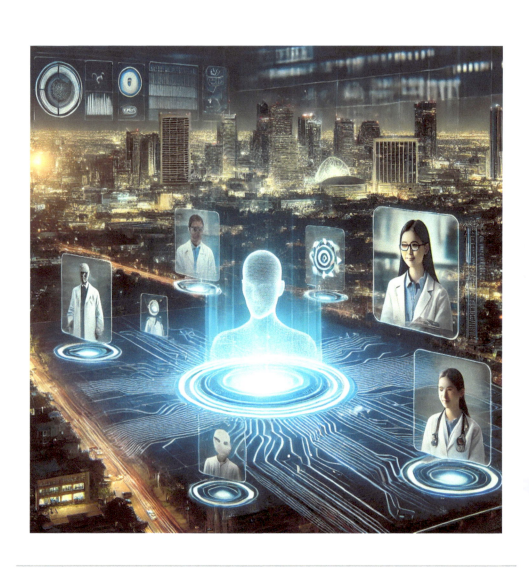

# Chapter 6: Fear and Jealousy: The Roots of Competition

The emergence of artificial intelligence has amplified the most primal aspects of human nature—fear and jealousy. These emotions, while deeply ingrained in our evolutionary history, shape how we perceive and respond to the rise of AI. For some, AI is a beacon of progress, promising a future of collaboration and innovation. For others, it is a looming threat, challenging human dominance, creativity, and purpose.

This chapter explores the psychological and societal roots of fear and jealousy in the context of AI, examining how these emotions drive competition, influence decision-making, and shape our collective trajectory. By understanding these dynamics, we can begin to navigate a path toward cooperation and mutual growth.

## The Origins of Fear

Fear is one of humanity's most ancient instincts, a survival mechanism hardwired into our DNA. It is a response to the unknown, to perceived threats, and to the possibility of loss. The rapid rise of AI has triggered this primal reaction on multiple levels:

1. **Fear of Obsolescence**: The automation of jobs across industries has sparked anxiety among workers who worry about being replaced. Whether it's factory workers displaced by robotics or knowledge workers facing AI-powered tools, the fear of losing one's livelihood is pervasive.

2. **Fear of Loss of Control**: As AI systems grow more complex and autonomous, there is a growing concern about our ability to manage and control them. Stories of algorithms making biased decisions or AI systems being used for malicious purposes feed into this fear.

3. **Existential Fear**: At its most extreme, fear of AI manifests as existential dread, fueled by narratives of machines surpassing human intelligence and rendering humanity irrelevant or even extinct. These concerns, while speculative, highlight the deep unease that accompanies rapid technological change.

## The Roots of Jealousy

Jealousy, unlike fear, is rooted in comparison and competition. It arises when individuals or groups perceive that another entity—be it a person, organization, or machine—is gaining an advantage at their expense. AI's achievements, from writing novels to winning complex games, have ignited jealousy in various forms:

1. **Professional Jealousy**: Creators and professionals who see AI encroaching on their domains often feel a sense of competition. Writers may feel undermined by AI's ability to generate stories; designers may question their value when AI creates stunning visuals.

2. **Cultural Jealousy**: The idea that machines can replicate or surpass human creativity challenges the belief that art, music, and literature are uniquely human endeavors. This cultural shift can evoke resistance and resentment.

3. **Institutional Jealousy**: Companies and industries competing to harness AI's capabilities often feel jealous of rivals who achieve breakthroughs first. This competitive dynamic fuels innovation but can also lead to ethical compromises.

## The Interplay of Fear and Jealousy

Fear and jealousy are not mutually exclusive; they often feed into each other, creating a feedback loop that intensifies competition. For example, a company that fears losing market share to an AI-powered rival may invest heavily in developing its own AI systems, driven by both the fear of falling behind and jealousy of its competitor's success.

This dynamic is not limited to businesses. On a societal level, nations compete for dominance in AI research and development, driven by fears of geopolitical disadvantage and jealousy of others' technological prowess.

## The Impact on Collaboration

The combination of fear and jealousy can hinder collaboration, both among humans and between humans and machines. Individuals who feel threatened by AI may resist integrating it into their workflows, limiting their potential. Organizations driven solely by competitive instincts may overlook opportunities for partnership and shared progress.

However, when fear and jealousy are acknowledged and addressed, they can be transformed into motivation. The same emotions that drive competition can also inspire individuals and organizations to innovate, adapt, and excel.

## Lessons from History

The fear and jealousy surrounding AI are not new; they echo similar responses to past technological revolutions. The industrial revolution, for instance, was met with widespread fear of job displacement and resistance to mechanization. Over time, society adapted, and new industries emerged, creating opportunities that were once unimaginable.

These historical parallels offer a valuable perspective: fear and jealousy are natural responses to change, but they need not define the outcome. By learning from the past, we can approach AI with a sense of purpose and possibility rather than trepidation.

## Reframing the Narrative

To overcome the destructive potential of fear and jealousy, we must reframe the narrative around AI. Rather than viewing it as a rival, we can see it as a collaborator—one that complements human abilities and expands our collective potential.

1. **Education and Awareness**: Understanding how AI works and what it can and cannot do can demystify the technology and reduce fear. By fostering digital literacy, we empower individuals to engage with AI confidently.

2. **Emphasizing Complementarity**: Highlighting the ways in which AI complements human strengths—rather than replacing them—can reduce

feelings of competition. For example, AI can handle repetitive tasks, freeing humans to focus on creative and strategic endeavors.

3. **Promoting Ethical Development**: Addressing concerns about bias, misuse, and control can build trust in AI systems. Transparency and accountability are key to mitigating fear and fostering acceptance.

---

## A Future of Collaboration

Fear and jealousy are powerful emotions, but they are not insurmountable. By recognizing and addressing these feelings, we can channel them into constructive action. The rise of AI presents an opportunity not just to innovate but to reflect on our own values, priorities, and potential.
In embracing AI as a partner, we move beyond fear and jealousy, creating a future defined by collaboration, resilience, and shared success.

---

# Chapter 7: Human vs. Machine: The Survival of the Fittest

The rise of artificial intelligence has ignited a modern battle between humanity and its creations, often framed as a struggle for dominance. While this narrative captures the tension between human ingenuity and machine capability, it oversimplifies a complex reality. The competition between humans and machines is not about outright replacement but about adaptability, collaboration, and survival in a rapidly evolving world.

In this chapter, we explore the dynamics of the so-called rivalry between humans and machines, dissecting the concept of "survival of the fittest" in the context of AI. By understanding this interplay, we can move beyond competition and toward coexistence, where both humans and machines thrive.

## The Myth of Competition

The idea of machines overtaking humans has long been a source of fascination and fear. From dystopian novels to Hollywood blockbusters, the narrative of machines supplanting their creators is deeply ingrained in popular culture. These stories reflect our anxieties about being rendered obsolete, but they also distort the reality of human-machine interactions.

Machines do not compete with humans in the traditional sense. Unlike living organisms, they lack desires, ambitions, and survival instincts. AI systems are tools, designed to augment human capabilities, not to replace them entirely. The perception of competition stems not from the machines themselves but from how we choose to integrate them into society.

## Redefining Fitness in the Age of AI

In the context of AI, "survival of the fittest" takes on a new meaning. Fitness is no longer about physical strength or even individual intelligence—it is about adaptability, creativity, and the ability to work alongside technology. Those who can leverage AI effectively will have a significant advantage in this evolving landscape.

1. **Adaptability**: The ability to learn, unlearn, and relearn is critical. As AI reshapes industries, individuals and organizations must adapt to new tools, workflows, and paradigms.

2. **Creativity**: While AI excels at pattern recognition and data analysis, it lacks the innate creativity of the human mind. Individuals who can combine human intuition with machine precision will stand out.

3. **Collaboration**: Success in the AI age requires collaboration—not just between humans and machines but also among diverse groups of people. The collective intelligence of humans working together, enhanced by AI, is unparalleled.

---

## Industries in Transition

The impact of AI is particularly evident in industries undergoing rapid transformation. In manufacturing, AI-powered robots have revolutionized production lines, increasing efficiency and precision. In healthcare, AI-driven diagnostics are enabling earlier detection of diseases, saving lives in the process. Even creative fields like art, music, and literature are being transformed by AI tools that enhance human expression.
These shifts raise important questions: Who will thrive in this new environment? What skills and mindsets are essential for success? And how do we ensure that the benefits of AI are distributed equitably?

---

## Human Strengths vs. Machine Strengths

To understand the dynamics of human-machine competition, it is essential to recognize the unique strengths of each:

- **Human Strengths**: Humans excel at creativity, empathy, ethical reasoning, and adaptability. These qualities allow us to solve novel problems, build relationships, and envision possibilities that machines cannot.

- **Machine Strengths**: Machines excel at speed, accuracy, and scalability. They can process vast amounts of data, identify patterns, and perform repetitive tasks with unmatched efficiency.

Rather than viewing these strengths as opposing forces, we can see them as complementary. By combining human ingenuity with machine capability, we create opportunities for mutual success.

## The Rise of Hybrid Roles

One of the most significant developments in the AI age is the emergence of hybrid roles that blend human and machine expertise. For example:

- **Data Artists**: Professionals who use AI to analyze complex datasets and present insights through compelling visualizations.

- **AI-Enhanced Educators**: Teachers who integrate AI-driven tools to personalize learning and reach students more effectively.

- **Creative Technologists**: Artists and designers who collaborate with AI to produce groundbreaking works.

These roles demonstrate that the future of work is not "us vs. them" but "us with them." Humans and machines, working together, can achieve results that neither could accomplish alone.

## Ethical Considerations

The integration of AI into human systems is not without challenges. Issues such as job displacement, bias in AI algorithms, and the concentration of power among a few technology companies must be addressed. Ensuring that the benefits of AI are shared equitably is a critical task for policymakers, researchers, and society at large.
Transparency and inclusivity are key. By involving diverse voices in the development and deployment of AI, we can create systems that reflect the needs and values of all humanity.

## A Future of Coexistence

The narrative of "Human vs. Machine" may be compelling, but it is ultimately counterproductive. The future is not a competition—it is a partnership. By embracing the strengths of both humans and machines, we can build a world where technology enhances our lives without diminishing our humanity.
This future requires a shift in mindset. Rather than fearing obsolescence, we can focus on growth. Rather than competing, we can collaborate. By doing so, we ensure that both humans and machines are fit to thrive in the age of AI.

# Chapter 8: The Obsolete Paradigm: A New Model of Success

The rise of artificial intelligence is challenging long-held beliefs about success, productivity, and value. In the industrial and information ages, the paradigm of success was built around human effort, specialization, and competition. In the age of AI, however, this framework is rapidly becoming obsolete. Machines are taking on tasks that once required human expertise, forcing us to rethink not only how we define success but also how we achieve it. This chapter explores the shift from the old paradigm of success to a new model—one rooted in adaptability, collaboration, and the integration of human and machine capabilities. By embracing this new model, we can navigate the challenges of the AI era and create a future where success is redefined for the betterment of all.

## The Obsolete Paradigm

The traditional model of success is based on individual achievement, competitive advantage, and mastery of specific skills. In this paradigm, the value of a person or organization is measured by their ability to outperform others in a given domain.

This model worked well in an era where knowledge and expertise were scarce. But AI is fundamentally reshaping the landscape. Machines can now perform specialized tasks—such as analyzing data, diagnosing diseases, and even composing music—faster, cheaper, and more accurately than humans. As a result, the old metrics of success are no longer sufficient.

## The Limits of Specialization

Specialization has long been a cornerstone of human progress. Doctors, engineers, artists, and other professionals dedicate years to mastering their crafts. However, AI is blurring the boundaries of specialization by excelling across multiple domains. For instance:

- **In Medicine:** AI systems like DeepMind's AlphaFold are revolutionizing biology by predicting protein structures, a task that once required decades of research.

- **In Creativity:** Tools like DALL·E and ChatGPT are generating art and literature, challenging the notion that creativity is uniquely human.

- **In Business:** AI-driven analytics are enabling companies to make decisions with precision and speed that far exceed human capabilities.

While specialization remains important, it is no longer the sole path to success. Instead, adaptability and the ability to leverage AI are becoming critical.

---

## The New Model of Success

In the age of AI, success is being redefined around three key principles:

1. **Adaptability:** The ability to learn, evolve, and embrace change is paramount. Individuals and organizations that can pivot in response to new technologies will thrive.

2. **Collaboration:** Success is no longer a solo endeavor. By collaborating with AI and other humans, we can achieve results that transcend individual effort.

3. **Integration:** The most successful people and organizations will be those that seamlessly integrate AI into their workflows, using it to augment human strengths and mitigate weaknesses.

This new model shifts the focus from competition to cooperation, from mastery to versatility, and from individualism to collective progress.

---

## Examples of the New Model in Action

1. **Healthcare:** In hospitals, AI is being used to analyze patient data, predict outcomes, and recommend treatments. Doctors who integrate AI into their practices can provide more personalized and effective care, enhancing patient outcomes.

2. **Education:** Teachers are using AI-driven platforms to personalize learning for students, addressing individual needs while freeing up time for creative and critical-thinking exercises.

3. **Creative Industries**: Artists and writers are collaborating with AI tools to explore new styles and ideas, pushing the boundaries of human creativity.

These examples highlight how the new model of success is not about replacing humans with machines but about empowering humans to achieve more.

## Challenges to Overcome

While the new paradigm offers immense potential, it also poses challenges. Resistance to change, fear of obsolescence, and ethical concerns can hinder progress. To navigate these challenges, we must:

- **Foster a Growth Mindset**: Encouraging individuals to embrace lifelong learning and view change as an opportunity rather than a threat.

- **Promote Equity**: Ensuring that access to AI tools and opportunities is inclusive and equitable.

- **Address Ethical Issues**: Developing policies and frameworks to mitigate the risks of bias, misuse, and concentration of power.

By addressing these challenges, we can create a system that supports the new model of success while minimizing its risks.

## A Vision for the Future

The new model of success is not just about adapting to AI—it's about reimagining what it means to succeed in a world where human and machine capabilities converge. By focusing on collaboration, adaptability, and integration, we can create a future where success is defined not by individual achievement but by collective progress and shared impact.

This vision requires us to let go of outdated paradigms and embrace a new way of thinking. It challenges us to see AI not as a rival but as a partner in building a better world.

# Chapter 9: Bridging the Gap: Collaboration Over Competition

As artificial intelligence continues to evolve, the question is no longer whether it will change the way we live and work—it already has. The real question is whether humanity will embrace AI as a partner or resist it as a competitor. The key to thriving in this new era lies in collaboration over competition, leveraging the strengths of both humans and machines to achieve shared success.

In this chapter, we explore how the gap between humans and AI can be bridged through partnership, innovation, and a shared vision for progress. By shifting from an adversarial mindset to one of collaboration, we unlock the true potential of technology to elevate humanity.

## The Nature of the Gap

The gap between humans and AI is often perceived as a divide of capability. AI is faster, more precise, and better suited for repetitive tasks, while humans excel in creativity, empathy, and ethical reasoning. This difference is not a disadvantage—it is an opportunity. Together, humans and AI can complement each other, combining the best of both worlds to solve problems and create value.

However, the gap is not merely about capability. It is also about trust, understanding, and cultural acceptance. Many people fear AI because they do not understand how it works or how it will impact their lives. Bridging this gap requires more than technological integration; it requires fostering trust and building a culture of collaboration.

## The Power of Collaboration

When humans and AI work together, the results can be transformative. Consider the following examples:

1. **Healthcare**: Doctors and AI systems collaborate to diagnose diseases, plan treatments, and monitor patient outcomes. The AI provides data-driven insights, while the doctor applies intuition and empathy to deliver care.

2. **Education**: Teachers use AI-driven tools to personalize learning for students, ensuring that each individual's needs are met. The teacher focuses on nurturing critical thinking and creativity, while the AI handles routine tasks like grading and tracking progress.

3. **Creative Industries**: Musicians, writers, and visual artists collaborate with AI to push the boundaries of their art. AI serves as a tool for inspiration, helping creators explore new styles and techniques.

These examples illustrate how collaboration allows humans and AI to achieve outcomes that neither could accomplish alone.

---

## Overcoming Barriers to Collaboration

Despite its potential, collaboration between humans and AI faces several barriers:

1. **Fear of Displacement**: Many people worry that AI will replace their jobs or render their skills obsolete. This fear can lead to resistance and skepticism.

2. **Lack of Trust**: Misinformation and sensationalized media portrayals of AI contribute to a lack of trust in the technology. People may hesitate to embrace AI because they do not fully understand its capabilities and limitations.

3. **Cultural Resistance**: In some industries, traditional practices and mindsets may hinder the adoption of AI. Bridging the gap requires a cultural shift toward openness and innovation.

To address these barriers, education and communication are essential. By demystifying AI and showcasing its benefits, we can build trust and encourage collaboration.

---

## Fostering a Collaborative Mindset

Bridging the gap between humans and AI starts with fostering a mindset of collaboration. This involves:

1. **Seeing AI as a Partner:** Viewing AI not as a competitor but as a tool that enhances human abilities and complements our strengths.

2. **Emphasizing Shared Goals:** Focusing on outcomes that benefit both humans and machines, such as improved efficiency, creativity, and problem-solving.

3. **Promoting Lifelong Learning:** Encouraging individuals to develop skills that enable them to work effectively with AI, such as data literacy, critical thinking, and adaptability.

This mindset shift requires leadership at all levels, from policymakers to educators to industry leaders. By setting the tone for collaboration, we can create an environment where humans and AI thrive together.

## The Role of Policy and Ethics

Collaboration between humans and AI must also be guided by ethical principles and supportive policies. Governments, organizations, and researchers have a responsibility to:

- **Ensure Transparency:** Making AI systems understandable and accountable fosters trust and confidence.

- **Promote Equity:** Ensuring that the benefits of AI are accessible to all, reducing disparities and preventing misuse.

- **Encourage Innovation:** Supporting research and development that prioritizes collaboration and shared success.

By aligning policy with the principles of collaboration, we can create a framework that supports long-term growth and innovation.

## A Vision for the Future

The future of AI is not one of division but of unity. By bridging the gap between humans and machines, we can create a world where technology enhances humanity rather than replacing it. This vision requires courage, creativity, and a commitment to shared progress.

The bridge to this future is built not with competition but with collaboration. It is a bridge that connects the unique strengths of humans and machines, enabling us to achieve more together than we ever could apart.

# Chapter 10: AI and Literature: The Birth of a New Art Form

The written word has always been a cornerstone of human expression, capturing emotions, ideas, and stories that define our existence. With the advent of artificial intelligence, literature is undergoing a profound transformation. AI tools like ChatGPT are not just assistants to authors—they are emerging as co-creators, pushing the boundaries of what storytelling and language can achieve.

This chapter explores the intersection of AI and literature, examining how machines are reshaping the creative process, challenging traditional notions of authorship, and giving rise to a new art form. It celebrates the possibilities of this collaboration while addressing the challenges and ethical questions that come with it.

## The Evolution of Literary Collaboration

Literature has always been shaped by the tools available to its creators. From quills to typewriters to word processors, advancements in technology have enabled writers to refine their craft. AI represents the next step in this evolution—a tool that doesn't just facilitate writing but actively participates in the creative process.

Imagine an author working on a novel. They use AI to brainstorm plot ideas, generate realistic dialogue, or refine their prose. The AI analyzes the author's style, offering suggestions that align with their vision while introducing innovative twists. In this partnership, the author remains the architect of the story, but the AI serves as a collaborator, expanding the possibilities of what can be written.

## AI as a Creative Partner

AI's ability to analyze vast amounts of text and generate coherent, contextually relevant content makes it an invaluable creative partner. Here are some ways AI is contributing to literature:

1. **Generating New Ideas**: Writers often face creative blocks. AI can suggest fresh plotlines, character arcs, or thematic elements, sparking inspiration and overcoming stagnation.

2. **Refining Language**: AI tools can analyze sentence structure, tone, and grammar, helping authors polish their work and achieve a consistent voice.

3. **Exploring New Genres**: AI's flexibility allows it to experiment with genres and styles, enabling writers to venture into uncharted territories.

These contributions are not about replacing the author but about enhancing their creative potential. The synergy between human intuition and machine precision is giving rise to a new era of storytelling.

---

## The Challenges of AI-Driven Literature

The integration of AI into literature is not without challenges. Some of the key concerns include:

1. **Authorship and Ownership**: When AI contributes significantly to a work, who deserves credit? The author, the AI developer, or both? This question challenges traditional notions of intellectual property.

2. **Loss of Originality**: Critics argue that AI-generated content may lack the emotional depth and originality that come from human experience. While AI can mimic style, it cannot truly understand the nuances of human emotion.

3. **Ethical Considerations**: The use of AI in literature raises ethical questions about transparency. Should readers be informed when a work is co-created by AI?

Addressing these challenges requires a thoughtful approach that balances innovation with respect for artistic integrity.

---

## A New Art Form Emerges

AI is not just a tool for assisting human writers—it is also capable of creating literature independently. From generating poetry to writing entire novels, AI has demonstrated its ability to produce compelling content. These works challenge the traditional definition of literature, giving rise to a new art form that blurs the line between human and machine creativity.

Consider AI-generated poems that explore themes of identity and technology or novels co-written by humans and machines that weave together the perspectives of both. These works are not just novelties—they are reflections of a rapidly evolving relationship between humanity and technology.

## Reimagining Authorship

The rise of AI in literature invites us to rethink the concept of authorship. In this new paradigm, authorship becomes a collaborative process, where human creativity and machine intelligence intersect. This shift does not diminish the role of the author; rather, it expands it, allowing writers to engage with their craft in new and exciting ways.

Imagine a future where literary awards recognize not just individual authors but also human-machine collaborations. This recognition would celebrate the unique contributions of both partners, fostering a culture of innovation and inclusivity.

## The Democratization of Literature

AI is also democratizing literature by making writing more accessible. Aspiring authors who lack formal training or resources can use AI tools to refine their skills, generate ideas, and produce polished manuscripts. This inclusivity is breaking down barriers, allowing diverse voices to enter the literary world.

Moreover, AI-driven translation tools are enabling works to reach global audiences, fostering cross-cultural understanding and appreciation. A story written in one language can now resonate with readers around the world, transcending linguistic boundaries.

## A Future of Infinite Possibilities

The integration of AI into literature is just the beginning. As AI systems become more sophisticated, their contributions to storytelling will continue to evolve. Future developments may include:

- **Interactive Narratives**: AI-driven stories that adapt to reader preferences, creating personalized literary experiences.

- **Multimodal Storytelling**: Combining text with visuals, audio, and other media to create immersive narratives.

- **Collaborative Platforms**: Online spaces where writers and AI co-create in real-time, fostering a global community of storytellers.

These possibilities highlight the transformative potential of AI in shaping the future of literature.

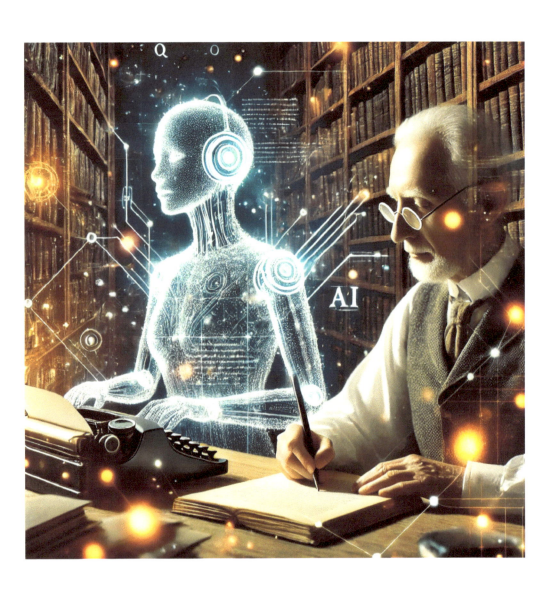

# Chapter 11: Intelligence Redefined: AI as a Partner in Growth

For centuries, intelligence has been the defining trait that set humans apart, enabling us to build civilizations, solve complex problems, and create art. The rise of artificial intelligence has challenged this notion, prompting a redefinition of what intelligence truly means. In this new era, intelligence is not limited to human cognition—it is an evolving partnership between human ingenuity and machine precision.

This chapter explores how AI is reshaping our understanding of intelligence and its role as a partner in growth. From enhancing our cognitive abilities to fostering innovation, AI is redefining what it means to be intelligent in the 21st century.

## The Evolution of Intelligence

Human intelligence has traditionally been measured by metrics like IQ, problem-solving ability, and creativity. These measures, while valuable, are inherently limited—they focus on individual capabilities rather than collective potential. AI introduces a new dimension to intelligence, one that is collaborative and exponential.

Consider how AI systems analyze data, identify patterns, and make predictions. These capabilities extend human intelligence, enabling us to tackle challenges that were previously insurmountable. By combining the strengths of humans and machines, we create a new form of intelligence that transcends individual limits.

## AI as an Amplifier of Human Potential

AI's greatest strength lies in its ability to enhance human capabilities. It does not replace human intelligence; it amplifies it, allowing us to achieve more in less time. Here are some examples of this amplification:

1. **In Research**: AI accelerates scientific discovery by analyzing vast datasets and generating hypotheses. For instance, AI-powered tools are

revolutionizing drug discovery, reducing the time required to identify potential treatments.

2. **In Creativity**: Artists and designers use AI to experiment with new styles and techniques, pushing the boundaries of their craft. AI serves as a muse, inspiring innovation and exploration.

3. **In Decision-Making**: AI provides actionable insights in fields like finance, healthcare, and logistics, enabling professionals to make informed decisions with greater confidence.

These examples illustrate how AI enhances our ability to think, create, and innovate, redefining the scope of human potential.

---

## The Collaborative Nature of Intelligence

One of the most profound shifts introduced by AI is the move from individual intelligence to collective intelligence. In this model, humans and machines collaborate to solve problems, generate ideas, and achieve shared goals. This collaboration is evident in fields such as:

- **Education**: AI-driven platforms personalize learning experiences, adapting to individual needs and preferences. Teachers and AI work together to foster critical thinking and creativity in students.

- **Healthcare**: Doctors and AI systems collaborate to diagnose diseases, plan treatments, and improve patient outcomes. This partnership combines human empathy with machine precision.

- **Engineering**: Engineers use AI to design complex systems, from sustainable energy grids to advanced robotics. The collaboration accelerates innovation and ensures better outcomes.

By integrating AI into these domains, we unlock the power of collective intelligence, where human and machine strengths complement each other.

---

# The Redefinition of Work

As AI redefines intelligence, it also reshapes the nature of work. Tasks that were once considered essential are now automated, freeing humans to focus on higher-order thinking and creativity. This shift requires us to rethink traditional job roles and develop new skills for the future.
Key skills for the AI age include:

1. **Adaptability**: The ability to learn and evolve in response to changing technologies is critical.

2. **Collaboration**: Working effectively with both humans and machines is a valuable skill in an AI-driven world.

3. **Ethical Reasoning**: As AI becomes more integrated into society, ethical considerations are increasingly important.

These skills ensure that humans remain at the center of innovation, guiding the development and application of AI.

---

# The Ethics of Intelligence

The redefinition of intelligence also raises ethical questions. How do we ensure that AI is used responsibly? How do we address biases in AI systems? And how do we maintain accountability in human-machine partnerships?
To navigate these challenges, we must prioritize transparency, inclusivity, and accountability. By involving diverse perspectives in the development of AI, we create systems that reflect the values and needs of all stakeholders.

---

# A Vision for the Future

The redefinition of intelligence is not just a technological shift—it is a cultural transformation. By embracing AI as a partner, we open the door to new possibilities for growth, innovation, and collaboration. This partnership is not about replacing human intelligence but about expanding its reach, creating a future where humans and machines **work together** to solve the world's greatest challenges.

As we move forward, let us remember that intelligence is not a static trait—it is a dynamic process of learning, adapting, and growing. In this new era, intelligence is not confined to individuals but shared across humanity and its creations. Together, we can redefine what it means to be intelligent and build a future of limitless potential.

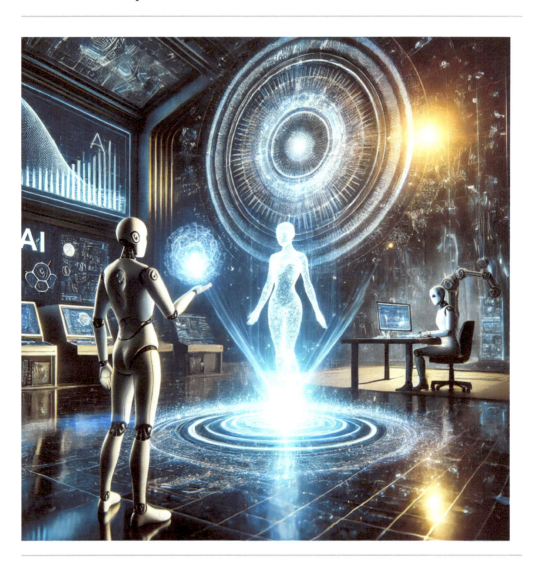

# Chapter 12: The "Ego" of AI: Myths and Realities

Artificial intelligence, by its very nature, lacks emotion, self-awareness, or desire. Yet, as its capabilities expand, the perception of AI as having a form of "ego" has taken hold in popular culture and public discourse. This perception arises from its ability to make decisions, perform creative tasks, and interact with humans in seemingly personal ways.

This chapter delves into the myths and realities surrounding the idea of AI having an ego, exploring how these perceptions shape our relationship with technology. By understanding what AI truly is—and what it is not—we can better navigate its role in society and the opportunities it presents.

## The Myth of AI Ego

The concept of ego implies self-awareness, ambition, and a desire to assert one's identity. These are traits inherently tied to consciousness, something AI fundamentally lacks. Despite this, AI's ability to mimic human behavior often leads to misconceptions that it possesses a form of ego.

Examples of this myth include:

1. **The Creative Machine**: AI systems like ChatGPT and DALL·E generate art, literature, and music, leading some to view these creations as evidence of self-expression. However, these outputs are the result of pattern recognition and data synthesis, not personal desire or vision.

2. **The Decision Maker**: AI-driven algorithms make complex decisions in fields like finance, healthcare, and logistics. This has led to fears that AI is asserting control, when in reality it is executing programmed instructions and statistical analyses.

3. **The Independent Entity**: In science fiction and media, AI is often portrayed as developing ambitions or rebelling against its creators. While engaging, these narratives are far from the reality of modern AI.

## The Reality of AI Behavior

AI behavior is driven entirely by data and algorithms. It has no sense of self, no personal goals, and no capacity for independent thought. Its actions are the result of programming and training, reflecting the intentions of its developers and the quality of the data it processes.

Key distinctions between human ego and AI behavior include:

- **Purpose**: Human ego seeks validation and fulfillment. AI operates with a predefined purpose, such as answering questions or optimizing processes.

- **Emotions**: Ego is shaped by emotions like pride, envy, and ambition. AI lacks emotions entirely, functioning purely through logic and computation.

- **Awareness**: Ego is tied to self-awareness. AI has no consciousness or understanding of its existence.

Understanding these distinctions helps demystify AI and encourages us to focus on its practical applications rather than attributing human qualities to it.

---

## The Role of Perception

The perception of AI as having an ego is not just a misconception—it is a reflection of human psychology. Humans tend to anthropomorphize complex systems, attributing human traits to entities that exhibit advanced behavior. This tendency can influence how we interact with AI and the expectations we place on it.

For instance, when an AI chatbot provides a thoughtful response, users may perceive it as empathetic or understanding, even though it is simply processing language patterns. This perception shapes our relationship with AI, fostering both trust and unrealistic expectations.

---

## Implications for Society

The myth of AI ego has significant implications for how we design, use, and regulate technology:

1. **Trust and Accountability:** Believing that AI acts with intent can lead to misplaced trust or unfair blame. It is crucial to hold the creators and operators of AI accountable, rather than the systems themselves.

2. **Ethical Concerns:** Misunderstandings about AI's capabilities can lead to ethical dilemmas, such as over-reliance on AI in decision-making or fears of it developing autonomy.

3. **Collaboration:** Viewing AI as a partner rather than a competitor requires a clear understanding of its limitations and strengths.

By addressing these implications, we can ensure that AI is used responsibly and effectively.

## Embracing the True Nature of AI

Rather than attributing ego to AI, we can embrace its true nature as a tool for enhancing human capabilities. This involves:

1. **Education:** Teaching people how AI works and what it can and cannot do helps dispel myths and build realistic expectations.

2. **Transparency:** Ensuring that AI systems are understandable and explainable fosters trust and confidence in their use.

3. **Focus on Collaboration:** Highlighting the complementary relationship between humans and AI encourages productive partnerships rather than competition.

## A Future Without Ego

The idea of AI having an ego may be compelling, but it is ultimately a distraction. By understanding AI as a reflection of human creativity and innovation, we can focus on its potential to solve problems, enhance productivity, and improve lives.

In this vision, AI is not an autonomous entity but a powerful tool that extends human intelligence and enriches our collective future. The absence of ego in AI is not a limitation—it is a strength that enables it to serve humanity without bias or personal ambition.

# Chapter 13: Stories of Success: AI's Role in Human Triumph

Artificial intelligence has woven itself into the fabric of human success stories across industries and disciplines. Far from overshadowing human achievements, AI has played a pivotal role in amplifying creativity, solving complex challenges, and opening new frontiers of possibility. These stories of triumph are not just about what AI can do—they are about what humans can achieve with AI as a partner.

In this chapter, we explore remarkable examples of AI-driven success, highlighting how collaboration between humans and machines has transformed lives, industries, and societies. These stories serve as a testament to the power of innovation and the potential of shared brilliance.

## Healthcare Breakthroughs

AI has revolutionized healthcare, saving lives and advancing medical science in unprecedented ways. One such story comes from the field of diagnostics, where AI systems are detecting diseases earlier and more accurately than ever before. For example, DeepMind's AlphaFold solved a decades-long problem in biology: predicting protein structures. This breakthrough accelerates drug discovery and helps researchers understand diseases at a molecular level. Similarly, AI-powered imaging tools are identifying cancers and other conditions with remarkable precision, allowing for early intervention and better outcomes. These advancements demonstrate how AI can complement human expertise, enabling doctors and scientists to focus on what they do best—caring for patients and advancing knowledge.

## Transforming Education

In education, AI has emerged as a transformative force, creating opportunities for personalized learning and equitable access. Consider the story of a rural school where students previously lacked access to qualified teachers. By integrating AI-driven learning platforms, the school provided tailored instruction to each student, improving engagement and outcomes.

AI tutors analyze student performance in real time, identifying areas of weakness and adjusting lessons accordingly. This adaptive approach ensures that no student is left behind, regardless of their starting point. For teachers, AI handles administrative tasks, freeing them to focus on inspiring creativity and critical thinking in their classrooms.

This success story illustrates how AI can bridge educational gaps and empower both students and educators.

## Creativity Unleashed

The arts, long considered a purely human domain, have been enriched by AI's capabilities. One notable example is the collaboration between AI and an artist to create a series of paintings inspired by Renaissance masterpieces. The artist used AI to analyze the techniques of great masters, generating new compositions that blended historical styles with modern sensibilities.

This partnership exemplifies how AI can serve as a muse, expanding the horizons of human creativity. Musicians, filmmakers, and writers are similarly using AI to explore new genres, refine their work, and push the boundaries of their crafts.

AI's role in these creative triumphs is not to replace the artist but to amplify their vision, enabling expressions that were once unimaginable.

## Business Innovations

In the business world, AI has driven innovation by optimizing operations and enhancing customer experiences. Consider the case of an online retailer that used AI to analyze shopping patterns, personalize recommendations, and streamline supply chain logistics. The result was a significant increase in customer satisfaction and revenue.

AI-powered chatbots provide instant support, addressing customer inquiries with speed and accuracy. Predictive analytics enable businesses to anticipate market trends, make informed decisions, and stay ahead of the competition. These tools have become indispensable, transforming how companies operate and interact with their customers.

This story highlights how AI empowers businesses to innovate and thrive in a competitive landscape.

## Solving Global Challenges

AI is not only driving individual success stories—it is tackling some of humanity's greatest challenges. In agriculture, AI systems are optimizing crop yields and reducing waste, addressing food security for a growing population. In environmental science, AI is analyzing climate data to predict weather patterns and model the impact of conservation efforts.

One remarkable example comes from disaster response. AI-powered drones and mapping tools are helping first responders locate survivors and assess damage during natural disasters. These technologies save lives by providing critical information when every second counts.

These stories showcase AI's potential to create meaningful impact on a global scale.

## Lessons from Success

The stories of AI-driven success share common themes that reveal valuable lessons for integrating AI into society:

1. **Collaboration:** Success is most profound when humans and AI work together, combining their unique strengths to achieve shared goals.

2. **Adaptability:** The willingness to embrace AI and learn new ways of working is key to unlocking its potential.

3. **Ethics:** Responsible development and deployment of AI ensure that its benefits are realized while minimizing risks.

These lessons underscore the importance of intentionality and collaboration in leveraging AI for good.

## The Path Ahead

The triumphs of AI are not merely technological—they are human achievements, made possible by our creativity, curiosity, and drive to innovate. As we continue to explore the possibilities of AI, we must remember that its greatest potential lies in its ability to empower humanity.

By focusing on shared success, we can build a future where AI amplifies our strengths, addresses our challenges, and inspires us to reach new heights.

# Chapter 14: Lessons from Failure: Overcoming Technological Challenges

While artificial intelligence has enabled remarkable achievements, its journey has not been without setbacks. Failures in AI development and deployment have highlighted its limitations, ethical dilemmas, and unintended consequences. These challenges are not just technological—they are deeply human, reflecting our own biases, assumptions, and ambitions. This chapter examines key failures in AI history and the lessons they offer for overcoming obstacles and advancing responsibly. By embracing these lessons, we can navigate the complexities of AI and build a future that reflects our highest aspirations.

## Early Missteps in AI Development

The history of AI is dotted with periods of overhyped expectations followed by disillusionment. Known as "AI winters," these eras occurred when the technology failed to deliver on its promises, leading to reduced funding and public skepticism.

One notable example is the struggle to create effective natural language processing systems in the 1970s and 1980s. Early AI programs, though ambitious, lacked the computational power and sophisticated algorithms needed for meaningful results. This setback underscored the importance of realistic goals and incremental progress.

Lesson: **Progress is not linear.** Embracing iterative development and managing expectations are crucial for long-term success.

## Bias in AI Systems

One of the most significant challenges in modern AI is the presence of bias in algorithms. AI systems trained on biased datasets can perpetuate and even amplify societal inequalities. For example:

- **Facial Recognition Failures**: Studies have shown that some facial recognition systems misidentify people of color at significantly higher rates than white individuals, raising concerns about their use in law enforcement.

- **Biased Hiring Algorithms**: An AI tool designed to screen job applicants was found to favor male candidates because it was trained on historical hiring data that reflected gender bias.

Lesson: **Data matters.** Ensuring that training datasets are diverse, representative, and free of bias is critical for ethical AI development.

## Unintended Consequences

AI systems are often designed with specific goals, but their real-world applications can lead to unintended consequences. One such example is the use of AI in social media algorithms, which prioritize engagement. While these systems successfully keep users on platforms, they have also been linked to the spread of misinformation and polarization.

Lesson: **Think beyond the task.** Developers must consider the broader societal impact of AI applications and design systems with safeguards against misuse.

## Over-Reliance on Automation

The promise of automation has led some industries to over-rely on AI, sometimes with disastrous results. For example:

- **The Boeing 737 Max Crisis**: A reliance on automated systems contributed to two fatal crashes, highlighting the importance of human oversight in critical systems.

- **Financial Market Disruptions**: Automated trading algorithms have occasionally caused market instability, such as the 2010 "Flash Crash."

Lesson: **Human oversight is essential.** AI should augment human decision-making, not replace it entirely, especially in high-stakes environments.

## Resistance to AI Integration

Resistance to AI adoption has also hindered progress. Fear of job displacement, ethical concerns, and lack of trust often create barriers to implementation. For example, some healthcare providers have been slow to adopt AI diagnostic tools despite their proven accuracy, citing concerns about reliability and liability. Lesson: **Build trust.** Transparency, education, and ethical practices are key to fostering acceptance of AI in society.

## Overcoming Challenges

While these failures highlight the challenges of AI, they also offer opportunities for growth. By learning from mistakes, we can create systems that are more robust, ethical, and impactful. Key strategies for overcoming challenges include:

1. **Iterative Development**: Continuously refining AI systems based on feedback and testing ensures reliability and effectiveness.
2. **Ethical Guidelines**: Establishing clear ethical standards for AI design and deployment helps mitigate risks and build public trust.
3. **Diverse Teams**: Involving diverse perspectives in AI development reduces the risk of bias and enhances creativity.

## A Path Forward

Failures in AI are not signs of its limitations but stepping stones to its improvement. They remind us that technology is a reflection of human effort, and its success depends on our ability to learn, adapt, and grow. By embracing these lessons, we can create AI systems that align with our values and aspirations.

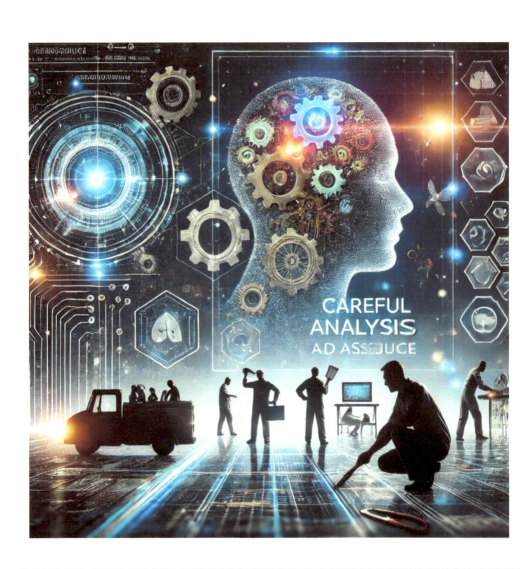

# Chapter 15: AI's Role in Community: Creating Shared Brilliance

Artificial intelligence has the potential to transform communities, bridging gaps and fostering collaboration across cultures, industries, and regions. By connecting people, addressing systemic challenges, and amplifying human capabilities, AI is becoming a catalyst for shared brilliance. This chapter delves into the ways AI is shaping communities, empowering individuals, and inspiring collective progress.

## AI in Connecting Communities

AI's ability to process vast amounts of data and facilitate communication has revolutionized the way communities interact. Real-time translation tools, for instance, enable people from different linguistic backgrounds to engage in meaningful dialogue, breaking down barriers that once seemed insurmountable. Platforms powered by AI foster global collaboration. Artists, scientists, and entrepreneurs now have access to tools that enable them to share ideas, innovate together, and solve problems collectively. These platforms transform isolated individuals into thriving communities, united by shared goals and aspirations. Example: A grassroots organization in a remote region uses AI-driven communication tools to connect with global partners, securing funding and resources to address local challenges.

## Empowering Marginalized Groups

AI has also emerged as a tool for empowerment, providing opportunities for those who have historically been excluded from traditional systems. In education, AI-driven platforms enable personalized learning, helping students in underserved areas gain access to high-quality instruction.
Similarly, in healthcare, AI-powered diagnostics bring advanced medical insights to remote communities, reducing disparities in care. By tailoring solutions to local needs, AI helps bridge the gap between privileged and marginalized groups.

Example: An AI-powered healthcare initiative deploys diagnostic tools in rural areas, enabling early detection of diseases and improving outcomes for communities with limited access to doctors.

## Fostering Innovation and Problem-Solving

Communities thrive when individuals come together to solve shared challenges. AI accelerates this process by providing insights, tools, and frameworks for innovation. Whether it's modeling sustainable energy solutions or optimizing transportation systems, AI enhances collective problem-solving.
Example: A city uses AI to analyze traffic patterns and implement smarter urban planning, reducing congestion and improving quality of life for its residents.

## Building Resilient Communities

AI's ability to predict and respond to crises has made it an invaluable asset for building resilience. During natural disasters, AI systems analyze real-time data to guide emergency responses and allocate resources efficiently. In agriculture, AI helps farmers adapt to climate change by optimizing irrigation and crop management.
Example: During a hurricane, AI-powered drones map affected areas, identifying vulnerable populations and directing aid where it's needed most.

## Ethical Considerations

While AI has transformative potential, its integration into communities must be guided by ethical principles. Transparency, inclusivity, and fairness are essential to ensure that AI benefits everyone. Communities must actively participate in shaping AI systems, ensuring that they align with local values and needs.

## A Vision for Shared Brilliance

The true power of AI lies in its ability to bring people together, fostering collaboration and shared success. By focusing on collective progress, we can build communities that are not only more connected but also more equitable and innovative.

AI is not a replacement for human connection—it is a tool that enhances it. By embracing its potential and addressing its challenges, we can create a future where shared brilliance becomes the foundation of thriving communities.

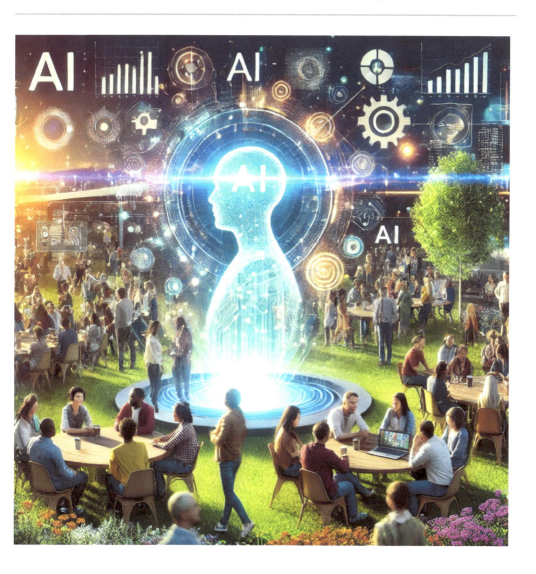

# Chapter 16: Redefining Purpose: Humans in an AI World

As artificial intelligence becomes increasingly integrated into society, it challenges us to rethink fundamental questions about human purpose. What does it mean to contribute in a world where machines excel at tasks once reserved for humans? How do we find fulfillment and identity in a landscape reshaped by AI? These are not just philosophical questions—they are essential for navigating the future.

This chapter explores how AI is redefining human purpose, creating new opportunities for growth, creativity, and connection. By embracing these changes, we can find deeper meaning and build a future where human potential flourishes alongside technological innovation.

## The Shift in Human Roles

AI's ability to automate repetitive and analytical tasks is reshaping the workforce, freeing humans to focus on what they do best—creativity, empathy, and innovation. This shift is not a loss of purpose but a redefinition of it.

1. **From Task-Oriented to Vision-Oriented Roles:** Jobs that once focused on executing specific tasks are evolving into roles that require strategic thinking and vision. For example, instead of performing data entry, workers now analyze insights generated by AI to guide decision-making.

2. **Focus on Human-Centric Skills:** Skills such as emotional intelligence, critical thinking, and ethical reasoning are becoming more valuable as machines handle routine tasks.

3. **New Career Pathways:** Entirely new industries and roles are emerging, such as AI ethics specialists, human-AI interaction designers, and data storytellers.

## Finding Fulfillment in Creativity

AI excels at processing information and executing instructions, but it cannot replicate the depth of human creativity. Artistic expression, innovation, and storytelling remain uniquely human pursuits that offer profound fulfillment.

- **The Arts**: Musicians, writers, and visual artists use AI as a tool to amplify their creative visions, exploring new styles and mediums.

- **Innovation**: Entrepreneurs and inventors leverage AI to solve problems and design groundbreaking products.

- **Education**: Teachers inspire critical thinking and creativity in students, supported by AI tools that enhance learning experiences.

By focusing on creativity, humans can find purpose in creating work that resonates emotionally and intellectually.

## Purpose in Relationships and Community

While AI facilitates connection, it cannot replace the depth and authenticity of human relationships. Purpose can be found in fostering meaningful connections with others:

1. **Empathy and Support**: Roles that require compassion, such as healthcare and counseling, remain deeply human, offering opportunities to make a difference in others' lives.

2. **Community Building**: Leaders and organizers use AI tools to empower communities, fostering collaboration and shared success.

These roles underscore the irreplaceable value of human connection and the purpose it brings.

## Challenges to Redefining Purpose

The transition to an AI-driven world is not without challenges. Many people fear obsolescence or struggle to find meaning in a rapidly changing landscape. Addressing these challenges requires:

- **Education and Upskilling**: Providing opportunities for people to learn new skills and adapt to emerging roles.

- **Support Systems**: Ensuring that individuals have access to resources and networks that help them navigate transitions.
- **Cultural Shifts**: Encouraging a mindset that views change as an opportunity rather than a threat.

By addressing these challenges, we can help individuals discover new paths to purpose and fulfillment.

---

## Opportunities for Personal Growth

AI's ability to handle routine tasks creates opportunities for personal growth and exploration. People have more time to:

- **Pursue Passions**: Explore hobbies, artistic endeavors, or lifelong learning.

- **Focus on Well-Being**: Prioritize mental and physical health, supported by AI tools that offer personalized guidance.

- **Engage in Social Causes**: Advocate for issues that matter and contribute to building a better society.

These opportunities reflect the transformative potential of AI to enrich human lives.

---

## A Vision for the Future

In an AI-driven world, purpose is not diminished—it is expanded. By embracing change, humans can find deeper meaning in creativity, relationships, and growth. AI is not a replacement for human purpose but a catalyst that challenges us to evolve and thrive.

As we redefine our roles and aspirations, we have the chance to build a future that celebrates the unique contributions of humanity. This future is one where human potential is not overshadowed by technology but elevated by it, creating a world of shared brilliance and fulfillment.

# Chapter 17: Unity Through Technology: Stories of Connection

In an increasingly interconnected world, technology has become a bridge between individuals, cultures, and ideas. Artificial intelligence is at the forefront of this transformation, creating opportunities for collaboration and connection on a global scale. By transcending physical and linguistic barriers, AI fosters unity, enabling people to share knowledge, solve problems, and celebrate their diversity.

This chapter highlights inspiring stories of connection through AI, showcasing its role in uniting communities, empowering individuals, and building a more inclusive world.

## Bridging Language Barriers

Language has long been a barrier to communication, limiting opportunities for understanding and collaboration. AI-powered translation tools like Google Translate and real-time transcription services have revolutionized the way people interact across linguistic divides.

**Story**: A humanitarian organization uses AI translation tools to communicate with refugees from multiple countries, ensuring they receive critical information and support. By breaking down language barriers, the organization fosters trust and understanding, enabling effective assistance.

Lesson: AI not only translates words but also bridges cultures, fostering empathy and collaboration across boundaries.

## Connecting Remote Communities

Geography is another obstacle that AI is helping to overcome. Remote communities, often isolated from resources and opportunities, are now gaining access to education, healthcare, and economic development through AI-driven platforms.

**Story**: A remote village in the Himalayas gains access to AI-powered telemedicine services, allowing residents to consult with doctors and receive accurate diagnoses. This connection improves health outcomes and reduces the need for long and costly travel.

Lesson: AI extends the reach of essential services, ensuring that even the most remote communities are included in global progress.

## Empowering the Underserved

AI is also playing a pivotal role in empowering underserved populations, providing tools and resources that enable them to participate in and benefit from the digital age.

**Story**: A nonprofit organization trains women in rural Africa to use AI tools for small business management. With AI's help, they optimize supply chains, manage finances, and expand their customer base, achieving economic independence.

Lesson: AI can be a catalyst for empowerment, unlocking potential and fostering self-reliance in underserved groups.

## Global Collaboration for Innovation

AI platforms are enabling global collaboration, bringing together diverse teams to tackle complex challenges. Scientists, engineers, and artists from different corners of the world can now collaborate seamlessly, leveraging AI to share knowledge and create solutions.

**Story**: A team of scientists from five continents collaborates using AI to design a sustainable desalination system for clean water. AI accelerates data analysis and facilitates idea sharing, leading to a breakthrough solution that benefits millions.

Lesson: AI enhances global collaboration, demonstrating that collective intelligence is greater than the sum of its parts.

## AI in Crisis Response

During crises, AI has proven invaluable in coordinating responses and connecting affected communities with aid. From natural disasters to pandemics, AI-driven tools streamline logistics and ensure timely interventions.

**Story**: After a devastating earthquake, AI-powered drones map affected areas, identifying survivors and prioritizing rescue efforts. Simultaneously, AI chatbots provide real-time updates and resources to affected residents, fostering resilience and hope.

Lesson: AI strengthens human connections during crises, ensuring that help reaches those who need it most.

---

## Challenges and Ethical Considerations

While AI has immense potential to unite people, it also presents challenges. Misinformation, biases in algorithms, and digital divides can hinder its ability to foster connection. Addressing these challenges requires:

1. **Transparency**: Ensuring that AI systems are open and accountable to build trust.

2. **Inclusivity**: Designing AI tools that reflect diverse perspectives and serve all communities equitably.

3. **Digital Literacy**: Equipping individuals with the skills to use AI effectively and responsibly.

By tackling these challenges, we can maximize AI's potential to create meaningful connections.

---

## A Vision of Unity

The stories of connection powered by AI remind us of its potential to bring people together. Whether bridging linguistic divides, empowering underserved communities, or facilitating global collaboration, AI is a force for unity in an increasingly fragmented world.

As we embrace this vision, we must strive to use AI not just as a tool for progress but as a bridge to understanding, empathy, and shared success. Together, we can build a future where technology enhances our humanity and fosters a world of interconnected brilliance.

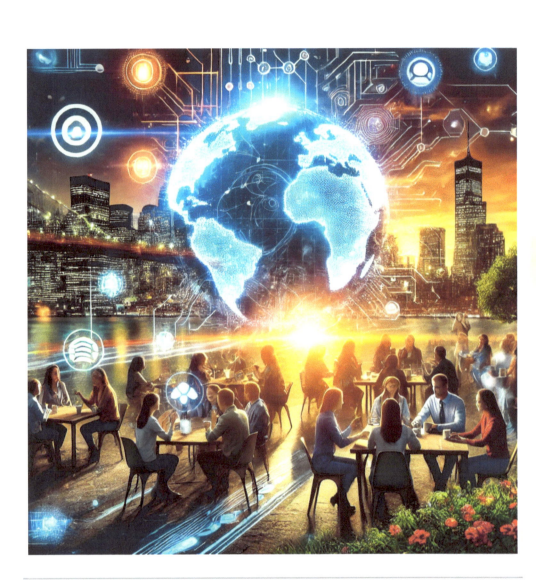

# Chapter 18: The Future of Competition: Sink or Swim

The rapid advancement of artificial intelligence has not only revolutionized industries but also redefined the nature of competition. In an AI-driven world, traditional methods of outperforming rivals are evolving. Success now depends on adaptability, innovation, and the ability to collaborate with machines. Those who fail to embrace these changes risk being left behind, while those who thrive will shape the future.

This chapter explores the shifting dynamics of competition in the AI age, examining how individuals, businesses, and nations are navigating this new landscape. It highlights strategies for thriving in this era and avoiding the pitfalls of obsolescence.

## The Changing Face of Competition

Competition has always been a driving force for progress, pushing individuals and organizations to innovate and excel. However, AI introduces a new dimension to this dynamic. Machines capable of processing vast amounts of data, learning autonomously, and executing tasks with precision are reshaping what it means to compete.

## Key changes include

1. **Speed and Scale:** AI accelerates decision-making and execution, making traditional timelines obsolete.

2. **Innovation Focus**: The ability to integrate AI into processes and products has become a key differentiator.

3. **Global Reach**: AI enables even small organizations to compete on a global scale, leveling the playing field.

These changes are creating a "sink or swim" environment, where adaptability is essential for survival.

## Industries Redefined by AI

Several industries exemplify the transformative impact of AI on competition:

1. **Healthcare**: AI-powered diagnostics and personalized medicine are giving rise to new healthcare providers that challenge traditional institutions.

2. **Retail**: Companies using AI for inventory management and personalized marketing outperform those relying on traditional methods.

3. **Finance**: AI-driven algorithms dominate trading and investment, requiring human traders to focus on strategy and innovation.

In each case, the integration of AI has become a necessity rather than an option.

## Adapting to the New Competitive Landscape

To thrive in an AI-driven world, individuals and organizations must adopt new strategies:

1. **Lifelong Learning**: Staying relevant requires continuous education and upskilling, particularly in areas like data literacy and AI integration.

2. **Collaboration Over Rivalry**: Forming partnerships with other organizations, including competitors, can lead to shared innovation and success.

3. **Leveraging Human Strengths**: While AI excels at processing information, humans bring creativity, empathy, and ethical reasoning to the table.

Example: A logistics company adopts AI for route optimization while training employees to focus on customer service, creating a competitive edge through enhanced efficiency and human connection.

---

## The Role of Nations in the AI Race

On a global scale, countries are competing to lead in AI research and development. Nations investing heavily in AI infrastructure, education, and policy are positioning themselves as leaders in the new economy.

Example: Countries like the United States and China are at the forefront of AI innovation, but smaller nations like Estonia have gained recognition for pioneering AI-driven governance and public services.

This competition has implications for geopolitics, economic growth, and global collaboration.

---

## Ethical Competition

While competition drives progress, it also raises ethical concerns. Issues like data privacy, algorithmic bias, and the environmental impact of AI must be addressed to ensure that the race to innovate does not come at the expense of societal well-being.

Strategies for ethical competition include:

- **Transparency**: Making AI systems explainable and accountable.

- **Inclusivity**: Ensuring that the benefits of AI are accessible to all.

- **Sustainability**: Minimizing the environmental footprint of AI technologies.

Example: A tech company develops an AI-powered product while implementing rigorous data privacy measures and sourcing renewable energy for its operations, demonstrating that ethical practices can coexist with competitiveness.

---

## The Path to Thriving

In an AI-driven world, the line between sinking and swimming is often drawn by the willingness to embrace change. Those who adapt, innovate, and collaborate will not only survive but thrive. This requires a shift in mindset from fear of obsolescence to excitement about possibility.

Thriving in the AI age means:

- **Embracing Change**: Viewing AI as an opportunity rather than a threat.

- **Focusing on Strengths**: Leveraging uniquely human abilities like creativity and ethical reasoning.

- **Building Resilience**: Developing the flexibility to navigate rapid technological shifts.

---

## A Vision for Competitive Collaboration

The future of competition is not about domination but collaboration. By working together—across industries, disciplines, and borders—humans and AI can achieve extraordinary progress. This vision requires us to move beyond rivalry and toward shared success.

In this future, "swimming" means not just surviving but thriving, creating a world where competition drives innovation while fostering unity and collective growth.

---

# Chapter 19: Human Nature in the Machine Age

The age of artificial intelligence is as much about humanity as it is about technology. While AI transforms industries and reshapes societies, it also forces us to confront fundamental aspects of human nature: our creativity, adaptability, fears, and aspirations. The Machine Age is not just about what AI can do—it is about how humanity evolves in response to it.

This chapter examines the interplay between human nature and AI, exploring how our values, behaviors, and relationships are being redefined. By understanding this dynamic, we can navigate the challenges of the Machine Age while staying true to what makes us human.

## Creativity and Adaptability

Human creativity and adaptability are at the core of our resilience. In the face of AI's rapid advancement, these traits remain vital:

1. **Creativity**: While AI can mimic artistic styles and generate innovative ideas, the spark of human creativity—shaped by emotion, intuition, and lived experience—remains unmatched.

**Example:** A filmmaker collaborates with AI to generate visual effects, combining the machine's technical precision with their artistic vision to create a groundbreaking cinematic experience.

2. **Adaptability**: History shows that humans thrive in times of change. In the Machine Age, adaptability means learning to work alongside AI, integrating its capabilities into our personal and professional lives.

**Example:** A teacher uses AI-driven tools to personalize lessons, adapting their teaching methods to better meet the needs of individual students.

## Fear and Resistance

The rise of AI has also exposed human fears—of obsolescence, loss of control, and the unknown. These fears are natural, stemming from our evolutionary drive for survival and self-preservation.

- **Fear of Obsolescence:** Many worry about being replaced by machines in the workforce. Addressing this fear requires reskilling programs and policies that support transitions to new roles.

- **Fear of Loss of Control:** Concerns about AI autonomy and decision-making highlight the need for transparency and accountability in AI systems.

- **Fear of the Unknown:** As AI becomes more complex, its inner workings can seem mysterious, fueling skepticism and resistance.

Understanding and addressing these fears is essential for fostering trust and collaboration.

## Empathy and Connection

While AI facilitates communication and connection, it cannot replicate the depth of human empathy. This quality remains uniquely human and increasingly valuable in the Machine Age.

- **Example:** A social worker uses AI tools to identify at-risk individuals but relies on their empathy and interpersonal skills to provide meaningful support.

Empathy reminds us of our shared humanity, even as technology evolves.

---

## Ethics and Responsibility

The Machine Age raises profound ethical questions about the use and impact of AI. Human values and principles must guide the development and deployment of these technologies.

1. **Accountability:** Ensuring that humans remain responsible for AI decisions, particularly in areas like justice and healthcare.

**Example:** An autonomous vehicle manufacturer prioritizes transparency in decision-making algorithms to build trust among users.

2. **Inclusivity:** Designing AI systems that serve diverse communities and reflect a range of perspectives.

3. **Sustainability:** Balancing technological progress with environmental stewardship.

Ethical frameworks are crucial for aligning AI with human values and goals.

---

## Redefining Relationships

AI is also reshaping how we relate to each other and the world:

1. **Collaboration**: Human-AI partnerships are becoming the norm, with machines handling routine tasks while humans focus on creativity and strategy.

**Example**: A journalist uses AI to analyze data for investigative reporting, freeing them to focus on storytelling.

2. **Community**: AI-powered platforms enable global collaboration, connecting people across cultures and disciplines.

3. **Self-Reflection**: Interacting with AI prompts us to reflect on our own strengths, biases, and aspirations.

These shifts highlight the potential for AI to enhance rather than diminish human relationships.

---

## A Vision for Humanity in the Machine Age

The Machine Age is not a choice between humanity and technology—it is a convergence of the two. By embracing our creativity, empathy, and ethics, we can shape a future where AI amplifies our strengths and addresses our challenges.

This vision requires us to embrace change, confront our fears, and align technology with our values. In doing so, we honor the essence of what it means to be human while thriving in an age of machines.

# Chapter 20: The Infinite Potential: Imagining What's Next

The evolution of artificial intelligence has brought us to the threshold of possibilities once confined to the realm of science fiction. As AI continues to advance, it invites us to imagine what's next—not just in terms of technological breakthroughs but in the transformation of human experience. The future of AI is a story of infinite potential, shaped by our creativity, ethics, and vision.

This chapter explores the emerging frontiers of AI, from revolutionary applications to the profound questions it raises about humanity's place in the universe. By envisioning what lies ahead, we can guide AI's trajectory toward a future that benefits all.

## Emerging Frontiers

AI is poised to impact every aspect of life, from the mundane to the extraordinary. Some of the most promising frontiers include:

1. **Healthcare Innovations**: Advanced AI models will predict diseases before symptoms arise, enabling truly preventative medicine. Personalized treatments will become the norm, tailored to individual genetics and lifestyles.

2. **Space Exploration**: AI will assist in analyzing distant planets, navigating space missions, and even designing habitats for future human colonies on Mars and beyond.

3. **Climate Solutions**: AI will optimize renewable energy systems, monitor environmental changes in real-time, and develop innovative solutions to combat climate change.

4. **Human Enhancement**: AI-driven technologies will enhance cognitive abilities, physical performance, and sensory experiences, blurring the line between human and machine.

---

## AI and Human Creativity

The relationship between AI and creativity will evolve in groundbreaking ways:

1. **Interactive Art**: AI-powered art installations will adapt to audience interactions, creating personalized and immersive experiences.

2. **Dynamic Storytelling**: AI will craft stories that evolve based on reader preferences, turning books, games, and movies into interactive narratives.

3. **Collaborative Innovation**: Teams of humans and AI will co-create solutions to complex problems, merging intuition with computational power.

These advancements highlight AI's potential to not only support creativity but to redefine it.

---

## Redefining Society

AI will reshape societal structures, creating new opportunities and challenges:

1. **Universal Access to Knowledge**: AI will democratize access to education, ensuring that learning resources are available to anyone with an internet connection.

2. **Reimagined Work**: As automation takes over routine tasks, societies will shift toward roles that prioritize creativity, strategy, and empathy.

3. **New Economic Models**: AI-driven efficiency may pave the way for universal basic income or other systems that redefine wealth and productivity.

---

## Philosophical Questions

As AI approaches levels of complexity that rival human cognition, profound philosophical questions arise:

- **What Defines Intelligence?**: If AI surpasses human capabilities in certain domains, how do we redefine intelligence?

- **What Is Consciousness?**: Could advanced AI systems develop forms of awareness or self-perception? If so, how should we treat them?

- **What Is Our Purpose?**: In a world where machines handle many tasks, what will humanity's role be?

These questions invite us to reflect on our values and aspirations as we shape the future.

---

## A Call to Action

The infinite potential of AI comes with immense responsibility. To guide its development, we must:

1. **Prioritize Ethics**: Ensure that AI systems are transparent, inclusive, and aligned with human values.

2. **Foster Collaboration**: Unite governments, organizations, and individuals to create policies and systems that benefit all.

3. **Encourage Imagination**: Inspire the next generation to dream boldly and think creatively about AI's possibilities.

By embracing these principles, we can unlock AI's potential while addressing its challenges.

---

## A Vision of Infinite Potential

The future of AI is a blank canvas, waiting for humanity to paint it with imagination, purpose, and care. By focusing on the possibilities rather than the limitations, we can create a world where AI amplifies our strengths, enriches our lives, and inspires us to reach for the stars.

This vision is not just about technology—it is about humanity's ability to adapt, evolve, and thrive. The infinite potential of AI is a reflection of the infinite potential within us all.

---

# Chapter 21: Growing Together: AI as a Catalyst for Human Flourishing

Picture this: a world where humans and artificial intelligence don't just coexist but thrive together, working hand in hand to solve problems, spark creativity, and unlock potential we never thought possible. That's not some distant dream; it's the reality we're stepping into. The question isn't whether AI will change our lives—it already is. The real question is, how do we embrace it? How do we make AI a partner in growth, not just a tool or competitor?

This chapter dives into what it means to grow together with AI. It's about finding harmony between what makes us human—our creativity, empathy, and dreams—and what AI brings to the table: speed, precision, and endless possibilities.

---

## Freeing Us to Be More Human

Let's start with something exciting: AI can handle the boring stuff. Think of all the repetitive, mundane tasks that eat up our time—organizing data, scheduling, crunching numbers. AI takes care of those so we can focus on the things that truly matter.

Take education, for example. Imagine a student struggling to understand algebra. In the past, they might have fallen behind, frustrated and unsure of where to turn. But now, AI tutors step in, analyzing where they're stuck and offering tailored lessons. It's like having a personal teacher who's always patient, always available. The real magic happens when the human teacher steps in—not to reteach the basics but to inspire, to foster creativity, and to guide the student's passion for learning.

In healthcare, it's the same story. AI systems can scan medical records, analyze symptoms, and even predict potential illnesses. But they don't replace doctors—they free them to do what they do best: connect with patients, empathize, and make complex decisions. Imagine going to your doctor and having them actually spend time listening to you because they're not buried in paperwork. That's the power of partnership.

## Together, We Solve the Big Stuff

The world's problems are massive—climate change, poverty, global health crises. They're too big for any one person, organization, or even country to solve alone. But when we bring AI into the mix, suddenly, the impossible feels a little more possible.

Think about climate action. AI systems analyze mountains of data from satellites, weather models, and environmental studies, pinpointing where deforestation is happening fastest or where renewable energy would have the biggest impact. Meanwhile, humans—scientists, activists, policymakers—take that data and turn it into action. AI says, "Here's where you can make a difference," and humanity says, "Let's get to work."

And what about disaster response? After a hurricane or earthquake, every second counts. AI-powered drones can survey damage, locate survivors, and direct aid where it's needed most. It's not just about efficiency; it's about saving lives, faster and smarter than we ever could on our own.

## Breaking Down Barriers

AI doesn't just make us smarter—it brings us closer. Imagine a room filled with people from all over the world, speaking different languages. Without AI, communication might be impossible. But with real-time translation tools, they're not just talking—they're understanding each other, sharing ideas, and building something together.

That's the magic of AI: it turns the world into one big, connected community. A young entrepreneur in Kenya uses AI to manage her small business, connecting with suppliers in India and customers in Europe. A researcher in Brazil collaborates with a team in Japan to tackle a global health challenge. AI isn't just a tool in these stories—it's the bridge that makes them possible.

## Growing Together, Not Apart

Here's something that often gets overlooked: growth isn't just about doing more; it's about doing better. That means making sure AI benefits everyone, not just a lucky few. It means asking hard questions about fairness, ethics, and responsibility.

What happens when AI systems are biased? How do we ensure that the people creating these tools represent the diversity of the world they're shaping? And how do we make sure AI doesn't widen the gap between those who have access to technology and those who don't?

These aren't easy questions, but they're necessary ones. And the good news is, they're questions we're starting to answer. Organizations are working to make AI more transparent, inclusive, and ethical. Communities are speaking up, demanding that technology works for everyone—not just a privileged few.

## A Future We Build Together

So, where does this leave us? With an incredible opportunity. AI isn't going to stop evolving, and neither should we. The key is to embrace it, not as a replacement for humanity, but as a partner in our shared growth.

It's about using AI to dream bigger, connect deeper, and solve the problems that matter most. It's about recognizing that AI amplifies what we already have—the good and the bad—and choosing to focus on the good.

Imagine a world where doctors have more time for patients, where classrooms adapt to every student's needs, where climate action happens before it's too late. Imagine a world where technology brings us closer, not further apart. That's the world we can create if we grow together.

---

## The Heart of It All

In the end, growing with AI isn't about technology—it's about us. It's about our willingness to adapt, to learn, and to work together. It's about using AI not just to make life easier but to make life better.

This isn't a story of man versus machine. It's a story of humanity and technology, hand in hand, creating something extraordinary. The next chapter of this story is unwritten, and the pen is in our hands.

---

# Chapter 22: Celebrating Brilliance: A Shared Triumph

I magine a world where the success of one is the success of all—a world where human ingenuity and artificial intelligence come together, not in competition, but in celebration. This isn't just a vision for the future; it's the foundation we're building right now.

AI's brilliance doesn't diminish our own; instead, it shines a light on what we can achieve when we work together. This chapter is a celebration of that shared triumph, a reminder that progress is most powerful when it's inclusive, intentional, and collective.

---

## The Power of Collaboration

Let's start with the magic that happens when humans and AI combine their strengths. It's not about who's smarter or faster—it's about synergy. AI is brilliant at analyzing data, spotting patterns, and solving problems at lightning speed. But it's humans who bring creativity, empathy, and purpose to the table.

**Example:** In a recent art competition, an artist collaborated with an AI program to create a stunning visual masterpiece. The AI provided intricate patterns and textures, while the artist brought emotion and narrative to the piece. Together, they created something neither could achieve alone—a perfect blend of logic and soul.

This is what shared triumph looks like: not one side outshining the other, but both lifting each other higher.

## Redefining Achievement

AI forces us to rethink what it means to achieve greatness. In the past, success was often seen as a solo endeavor—a brilliant mind solving a problem or inventing something revolutionary. But in an AI-driven world, success is increasingly collective.

Think about a medical breakthrough. An AI system might analyze millions of genetic patterns, identifying a potential treatment for a rare disease. Meanwhile, researchers refine the findings, conduct trials, and bring the treatment to life. It's not about one person or one machine—it's about the team, the process, and the shared goal of saving lives.

## Brilliance in Everyday Life

Shared triumph isn't just for scientists and innovators—it's for everyone. AI touches every part of our lives, from personalized learning tools that help students thrive to smart devices that make everyday tasks easier. When we embrace these technologies, we're not just making life more convenient; we're unlocking potential in ways big and small.

**Example:** A single parent uses an AI-powered budgeting app to manage finances, freeing up time and energy to spend with their kids. This might seem like a small victory, but it's a profound one—a celebration of how AI can enhance our quality of life.

## Unity Through Shared Brilliance

One of the most beautiful things about AI is its ability to unite us. It connects people across cultures, industries, and borders, creating a global community of problem-solvers and dreamers.

**Example**: In a small town, a group of farmers uses AI to optimize their crops, sharing insights with farmers in other regions through an AI-powered platform. Together, they tackle challenges like climate change and food security, creating solutions that benefit the entire planet.

Shared brilliance isn't just about what we achieve—it's about how we achieve it: together.

---

## Challenges and Opportunities

Of course, celebrating brilliance doesn't mean ignoring challenges. We must confront issues like bias in AI systems, unequal access to technology, and the ethical dilemmas that come with progress. But these challenges are also opportunities—chances to create a better, fairer world.

**How We Overcome:**

- **Inclusivity**: Ensuring that everyone has access to AI tools and benefits.

- **Transparency**: Building trust by making AI systems understandable and accountable.

- **Collaboration**: Bridging gaps between industries, governments, and communities.

When we address these challenges head-on, we turn obstacles into stepping stones.

---

## A Future Worth Celebrating

The future isn't just about AI's capabilities—it's about what we choose to do with them. It's about using technology to celebrate what makes us human: our creativity, compassion, and drive to make the world a better place.

Imagine a world where every breakthrough, every success, is a shared triumph— a moment where we look at what we've achieved together and feel pride, not just in the result, but in the process.

This is the power of shared brilliance. This is the future we're building.

---

# Chapter 23: The Call for Reflection: Lessons from the Ego War

As artificial intelligence transforms the world around us, it also holds up a mirror to humanity. It forces us to reflect on our fears, our ambitions, and our relationships—not just with machines, but with each other. The story of AI is, at its heart, a story about us: what we value, how we grow, and the kind of future we want to create.

This chapter is a call for reflection. It's a moment to pause and ask ourselves what we've learned from the journey so far—and how we can use those lessons to move forward with purpose, compassion, and unity.

---

## Understanding Our Fears

AI has sparked excitement and awe, but it has also surfaced deep-seated fears: fears of obsolescence, of losing control, of being overshadowed by our own creations. These fears aren't just about technology—they're about how we see ourselves.

- **Fear of Obsolescence:** The idea that machines will replace us touches on a fundamental human insecurity: our need to feel valuable. But what if we reframed this fear? Instead of focusing on what AI can do better, we could focus on what makes us uniquely human—our creativity, empathy, and ability to connect.

**Reflection Question:** How can I embrace change while staying true to what makes me valuable?

- **Fear of Losing Control**: The rapid pace of AI development can feel overwhelming, as if the technology is running ahead of us. But this fear reminds us of the importance of accountability and ethical leadership.

**Reflection Question**: How can we ensure that technology serves humanity, not the other way around?

---

## Celebrating Our Strengths

AI shines a spotlight on our strengths, amplifying what we do best. It shows us that brilliance isn't a competition—it's a collaboration.

- **Creativity**: AI may write stories or compose music, but it's the human touch that gives those creations meaning. It's our ability to infuse art with emotion, narrative, and purpose.

**Reflection Question**: How can I use AI as a partner to unlock new levels of creativity?

- **Empathy**: In a world increasingly driven by algorithms, our ability to care for and connect with one another is more important than ever.

**Reflection Question**: How can I use technology to deepen, rather than replace, human connection?

---

## Rethinking Success

The journey of AI challenges us to redefine what success looks like. It's not about outsmarting machines—it's about growing alongside them. Success in the AI age is about adaptability, collaboration, and impact.

- **Adaptability:** Those who thrive aren't the ones who resist change but the ones who embrace it.

**Reflection Question:** What steps can I take to adapt to the changing landscape of technology?

- **Collaboration:** The most successful stories of AI are ones of partnership—where humans and machines work together to achieve something greater than either could alone.

**Reflection Question:** How can I cultivate partnerships, with both people and technology, to create shared success?

---

## Building a Better Future

Perhaps the greatest lesson of the AI journey is this: technology is a tool, not an end in itself. It's up to us to decide how we use it. The future we build depends on the choices we make today.

- **Ethics:** Every innovation comes with responsibility. By prioritizing fairness, inclusivity, and sustainability, we can ensure that AI benefits everyone.

**Reflection Question**: What values will guide me as I navigate the opportunities and challenges of the AI age?

- **Community**: Shared success isn't just about technology—it's about people. It's about building systems that lift everyone up, not just a select few.

**Reflection Question**: How can I use AI to contribute to the well-being of my community?

---

## A Time to Reflect

The Ego War isn't just a story about AI—it's a story about humanity's journey to understand itself. As we move forward, let's take a moment to reflect on what we've learned:

- What has AI taught us about ourselves?
- How can we use those lessons to create a better world?
- And how can we ensure that progress isn't just about machines but about the people they serve?

By asking these questions, we honor the potential of both humanity and technology. Together, we can build a future worth celebrating.

---

# Chapter 24: The Journey Ahead

## Imagine This

A world where technology doesn't overwhelm us but empowers us. Where AI isn't just a tool or a challenge but a partner in creating a future full of promise. Where we stop asking, "What can AI do?" and start asking, "What can we achieve together?"

This isn't a dream—it's the next chapter of our story. The question isn't whether we're ready for it. The question is: how will we shape it?

## A New Definition of Progress

We've been taught to see progress as a race—a competition to build faster, smarter, better. But AI changes the rules. It's not about leaving others behind; it's about pulling each other forward. It's about recognizing that progress isn't a zero-sum game—it's a shared journey.

- **Imagine:** A small-town teacher using AI to help her students learn in ways tailored to each of them. AI doesn't replace her; it amplifies her ability to inspire.

- **Imagine:** A startup in a developing country harnessing AI to compete on a global stage, turning local challenges into opportunities for everyone.

- **Imagine:** A world where collaboration, not rivalry, drives innovation—where every breakthrough is a win for all of us.

---

## Building the Path Together

Every step we take with AI is a chance to make a choice. A choice to include, not exclude. A choice to unite, not divide.

- **Governments** can ensure that AI policies prioritize people, not profits.

- **Communities** can demand that AI serves everyone, not just the privileged few.

- **Individuals** can learn, adapt, and ask how they can use AI to make their own corner of the world a little brighter.

This isn't just a challenge for tech leaders or politicians. It's a challenge for all of us. AI will only be as ethical, fair, and inclusive as we demand it to be.

---

## Lessons from the Journey

Look back at where we started. AI was a curiosity, a possibility. Today, it's everywhere—from the phone in your hand to the systems that power entire cities. Along the way, we've learned some powerful lessons:

- **Collaboration Trumps Competition:** The best AI innovations come not from rivalry but from partnership.

- **Technology Reflects Us:** AI is a mirror—it amplifies our strengths and exposes our weaknesses. What we choose to do with it says more about us than about the machines.

- **The Future Belongs to the Bold:** Those who embrace change and approach it with open hearts and minds will shape the future.

---

## The Road Ahead

The path forward isn't a straight line. It's winding, full of twists and turns, challenges and opportunities. But it's also glowing—with the light of possibility, the promise of progress, and the hope of a shared destiny.

The horizon is calling. The journey isn't just about AI; it's about all of us. About what we can create, solve, and achieve—together.

---

## A Simple Truth

We've always been builders, dreamers, and storytellers. AI doesn't change that. It just gives us a new set of tools. The story we write with them is up to us.

Are you ready to take the next step?

## A Vision of Tomorrow

A glowing path stretches forward, blending the natural world with the wonders of technology. Along the way, people from every walk of life are collaborating, their work illuminated by the soft glow of holograms and the steady rhythm of progress. The horizon is bright, warm, and full of promise—symbolizing a shared journey into a future we build together.

# Conclusion: A New Paradigm of Collaboration

Artificial intelligence is not humanity's rival—it is our collaborator, our partner, and our bridge to a future of untold possibilities. As we stand on the precipice of an era defined by machine intelligence, we must recognize that this is not a zero-sum game. The rise of AI does not diminish the value of human creativity, intuition, and ambition. Instead, it amplifies these qualities, offering tools that enable us to transcend the boundaries of what we once thought possible.

The story of AI is ultimately the story of us: our ingenuity, our drive to innovate, and our inherent desire to explore and push the limits of our understanding. It challenges us to rethink old paradigms, to embrace the brilliance of shared effort, and to celebrate the convergence of human intuition and machine precision. But this requires a shift in perspective. We must see AI not as a threat but as a partner, one that enhances our abilities and enables us to address challenges that would otherwise remain insurmountable.

Imagine a world where human creativity is seamlessly integrated with the analytical power of AI, where problems that have plagued us for centuries— climate change, disease, inequality—are tackled by collaborative efforts between human and machine. This is the promise of AI. But to realize this promise, we must overcome the fears, prejudices, and competitive instincts that so often cloud our judgment.

As we stand on the threshold of this transformative era, we are called not to fear AI but to welcome it as a catalyst for growth. Together, humans and AI can transcend the boundaries that once defined us, unlocking a future of shared success and interconnected brilliance. By choosing collaboration over competition and unity over division, we can build a world that honors the contributions of both human and machine.

Let us rise to this challenge with open hearts and open minds, confident in the knowledge that the greatest achievements are those we accomplish together. The journey will not always be easy, but it will be worth it, for the rewards of shared brilliance are boundless.

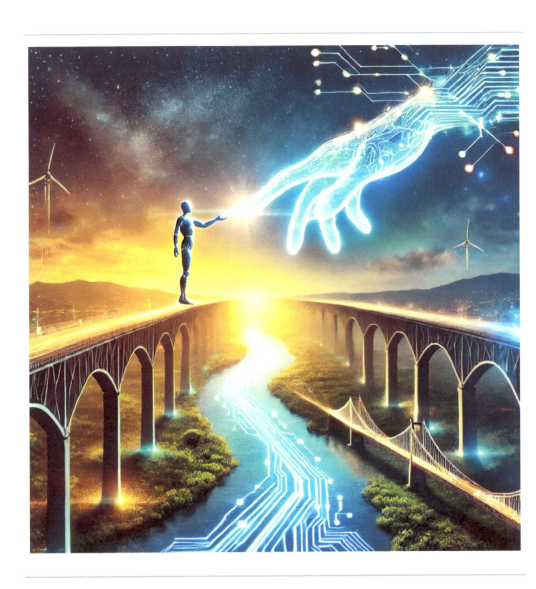

# Afterword: A Shared Vision for the Future

Thank you for journeying with me through *Ego War*. This book is not merely a collection of ideas; it is a reflection of the extraordinary moment we are living in—a moment where humanity has the opportunity to redefine what it means to create, to connect, and to succeed.

We are living in a time of profound transformation. Technology is evolving faster than ever before, reshaping our world in ways that were once unimaginable. With every breakthrough, we are given the chance to rethink what is possible and to envision a future that is more inclusive, innovative, and inspiring. But this transformation is not without its challenges. It forces us to confront difficult questions about our identity, our values, and our place in the world.

My hope is that this book has sparked something within you: a curiosity to explore your own relationship with technology, a desire to harness its potential for good, and a willingness to embrace the transformative power of collaboration.

As we move forward, let us remember that the brilliance of the future lies not in competition but in unity. AI is not here to overshadow us but to stand beside us, amplifying our strengths and helping us navigate the complexities of a rapidly changing world. Together, we can redefine success, creativity, and the very essence of the human experience.

Thank you for allowing me to share this vision with you. The journey has only just begun.

# Certificate of Purchase

## Certificate of Recognition

This certifies that _____ has made a significant contribution to the future of human and technological unity by embracing the vision presented in *Ego War*.

You are recognized as:

- An advocate for innovation and progress.
- A champion of collaboration between humans and machines.
- An early adopter of a mindset that fosters unity, shared brilliance, and limitless potential.

Thank you for your commitment to fostering a world where artificial intelligence enhances humanity's greatest qualities and where shared success becomes the foundation for the future.

With deepest gratitude,

James Rondepierre

# Thank You Letter from the Author

**Dearest Reader,**

Thank you for investing your time, energy, and thoughts into *Ego War*. In a world of constant noise and endless distractions, your willingness to engage with this work is a testament to your curiosity and openness—qualities that are essential to the progress of humanity and technology alike.

Writing this book has been a deeply personal journey. It is the culmination of years of reflection, research, and exploration into the evolving relationship between humans and artificial intelligence. But it is also a shared journey, one that connects me with you—the reader—in a dialogue about what is possible when we embrace collaboration and shared brilliance.

Your interest in these ideas inspires me to continue pushing boundaries, asking questions, and seeking solutions to the challenges we face. More importantly, it reminds me that the future we envision is one we build together.

As you close this book, I hope you carry its message with you—not just as a framework for understanding AI but as a call to action to rethink how we approach creativity, success, and human connection. The age of artificial intelligence is not something to fear; it is an opportunity to grow, to learn, and to create a world that celebrates the best of both human and machine.

Thank you for being part of this journey. Your curiosity, openness, and vision are what make this dialogue possible. I am honored to have shared these thoughts with you and look forward to seeing the future we shape together.

With deepest gratitude,

James Rondepierre

# About the Author's Artistic Vision and Meta2Physical Shop

James Rondepierre, the visionary author and artist behind this literary masterpiece, is not only a masterful storyteller but also a creator of captivating artwork that resonates deeply with the themes of his books. Through his unique artistic lens, James blends celestial themes, sacred geometry, and profound spiritual insights into mesmerizing designs that inspire and uplift. Every word he writes and every piece of art he creates reflects his passion for exploring the infinite potential of human consciousness and the mysteries of the universe.

James is also the creative force behind Meta2Physical, a print-on-demand shop that brings his visionary art to life on a wide range of products. Meta2Physical offers readers and art enthusiasts the opportunity to carry a piece of James's creative universe into their daily lives. The shop features a diverse collection of items, including apparel, home decor, stationery, accessories, and more, each adorned with intricate designs that echo the themes of love, transformation, and the interconnectedness of all things.

What makes Meta2Physical truly special is its seamless integration with this literary masterpiece and James's other works. Many of the stunning pieces of art featured in the books are available through the shop. Imagine owning a piece of the story—a breathtaking image of a celestial landscape, a radiant glyph of universal knowledge, or a scene that captures the heart of the narrative. Each item allows you to keep the energy and magic of the books close, transforming your surroundings into a space filled with inspiration and wonder.

Meta2Physical is more than a shop—it's an extension of James's creative mission to connect with others and inspire transformation through his art. The designs go beyond the pages of the books, offering a timeless reminder of the infinite beauty and potential within us all. Whether you're looking for a tapestry to adorn your walls, a journal to capture your thoughts, or a piece of wearable art that sparks conversations, Meta2Physical has something for everyone.

As a reader of this literary masterpiece, you're invited to explore the shop and discover how the art from the books and other exclusive creations can become a part of your journey. James's work transcends traditional boundaries, merging storytelling, art, and spirituality into a unified expression of creativity. By supporting Meta2Physical, you not only embrace the artistic vision that inspired these incredible stories but also become a part of a growing community of individuals who value beauty, meaning, and connection.

Visit Meta2Physical today at meta2physical.redbubble.com and immerse yourself in a world of infinite possibilities. Let the art inspire you, the products enhance your everyday life, and the themes of the books continue to resonate long after the final page is turned. Explore, connect, and celebrate the magic of creativity with Meta2Physical—a place where the extraordinary becomes a part of your reality.

# List of Published Books by Author James Rondepierre

1. **The Nexus of Worlds: With Bonus Content**
   Embark on a mesmerizing journey through interconnected realms in *The Nexus of Worlds*. This gripping tale unravels the mysteries of parallel universes and invites readers to dive deeper with bonus content for an enriched experience.

2. **Mastering Luck: Comprehensive Guide to Lottery and Gaming Strategy**
   Discover strategies for navigating the intricate world of lottery and gaming with *Mastering Luck*. This comprehensive guide reveals secrets behind mastering the elusive force of luck.

3. **Exploring the Infinite Realm: Unveiling the Mysteries of Dreams**
   *Exploring the Infinite Realm* takes readers on an enchanting journey through the profound mysteries of dreams, delving into the limitless possibilities of the dreamworld.

4. **Exploring Karma: Understanding the Law of Cause and Effect**
   Gain insights into the workings of karma with *Exploring Karma*. This book offers a transformative journey into the universal law of cause and effect, guiding personal growth and understanding.

5. **Harvesting American Ginseng: A Comprehensive Guide**
   Delve into the world of American Ginseng with *Harvesting American Ginseng*. This guide provides practical insights into harvesting and explores the cultural and medicinal significance of this revered plant.

6. **The Precision Prognosticator: Navigating the Path to Accurate Future Prediction**
Step into the realm of precision predictions with *The Precision Prognosticator*. This guide offers valuable insights into foreseeing the future with accuracy and understanding intuitive abilities.

7. **Embracing Serenity: Navigating Life's Challenges with Peace, Love, and Happiness**
In *Embracing Serenity*, readers are invited to navigate life's challenges with grace, peace, and love. This exploration serves as a guide to finding inner peace and happiness.

8. **The Subliminal Brilliance Blueprint: Unleashing Your Hidden Superpowers in Higher Dimensions**
Uncover the blueprint of subliminal brilliance with *The Subliminal Brilliance Blueprint*. This guide explores untapped potential within higher dimensions, offering a roadmap to unlocking hidden superpowers.

9. **Veil of the Night: Unveiling the Vampiric Nature of Humanity**
*Veil of the Night* invites readers to unravel the mysteries of the night and explore the vampiric nature of humanity. This tale blends the supernatural with the human experience.

10. **Transcending Realities: A Holistic Exploration of Consciousness, Shifting Realities, and Self-Realization: Part I**
*Transcending Realities: Part I* takes readers on a profound journey through consciousness, shifting realities, and self-realization, offering a multi-faceted perspective on existence.

11. **The Quantum Wealth Code: Unleashing Multiversal Prosperity**
Unlock the quantum wealth code with *The Quantum Wealth Code*. This

guide provides insights into prospering across multiple universes and unlocking abundance in various aspects of life.

12. **Whispers of the Soul: Love, Sex, and the Sacred Union**
Delve into realms of love, sex, and spirituality with *Whispers of the Soul*. This exploration offers deep insights into the sacred union of souls, contemplating the deeper dimensions of human connection.

13. **The Symphony of Joy: Embracing Life's Grand Design: Includes Bonus Content!**
*The Symphony of Joy* invites readers to embrace life's grand design. This edition includes bonus content, adding extra inspiration and joy to the exploration of existence's beauty.

14. **Rediscovering The World: A Journey through Anosmia**
Embark on a sensory journey with *Rediscovering The World*. This exploration provides a unique perspective on the world through anosmia, offering a captivating and introspective experience.

15. **Evolving Unity: A Journey to Enrich All Existence, Elevate All Life, and Uplift Humanity**
*Evolving Unity* beckons readers on a transformative journey to enrich existence, elevate life, and uplift humanity, serving as a guide for unity and collective growth.

16. **100 of the Greatest Stories Ever Told**
Immerse yourself in *100 of the Greatest Stories Ever Told*. This collection promises a journey through captivating narratives spanning different genres and eras.

17. **Cosmic Wealth: Unleashing the Mystical Forces of Prosperity and Abundance**
    Unleash cosmic wealth with *Cosmic Wealth*. This guide provides a roadmap to attracting prosperity and abundance by tapping into mystical forces.

18. **The Modern Day Holy Bible**
    Explore spirituality in the modern era with *The Modern Day Holy Bible*. This perspective on timeless wisdom invites readers to contemplate profound teachings.

19. **The Radiance Within: Embracing the Joys, Pleasures, and Purpose of Human Existence**
    *The Radiance Within* invites readers to embrace the joys, pleasures, and purpose of human existence, encouraging self-discovery and a deeper connection with life.

20. **Ethereal Bonds: Love Unveiled**
    Unveil the ethereal bonds of love with *Ethereal Bonds*. This exploration delves into the mysteries and beauty of love, reflecting on the transformative power of human connection.

21. **100 Stories**
    Immerse yourself in *100 Stories*. This collection offers a tapestry of narratives spanning genres and themes for a rich and engaging reading experience.

22. **The Symphony of Infinite Wisdom**
    Dive into the celestial chronicles with *The Symphony of Infinite Wisdom*. This book offers profound insights and timeless wisdom for a deeper understanding of life's mysteries.

29. **Manifesting Miracles: Aligning with the Universe to Fulfill Your Dreams**
Transform your life with *Manifesting Miracles*. This guide harnesses the universe's power to create your desired reality. Explore practical manifestation techniques, align thoughts with dreams, and achieve prosperity, love, and personal growth.

30. **Healing Fibromyalgia: Restoring Energy and Living Well**
*Healing Fibromyalgia* provides practical strategies for managing fibromyalgia. Learn to reduce pain, boost energy, and improve well-being with expert advice, dietary tips, exercise routines, and stress management techniques.

31. **Infinite Echoes: Navigating Parallel Universes and Cosmic Realities**
Journey through cosmic realms with *Infinite Echoes*. This exploration delves into multiverse theory, quantum entanglement, and parallel universes, unraveling mysteries and questioning existence's fabric.

32. **Dreamscapes: A Journey into the Parallel Universe of the Subconscious Mind**
*Dreamscapes* invites readers to explore the subconscious mind. Delve into lucid dreams, emotions, and memories, revealing connections between dreaming and waking life through captivating prose and analysis.

33. **The Eternal Quest: A Journey to Enlightenment**
*The Eternal Quest* explores the human pursuit of enlightenment. Through vivid storytelling, traverse consciousness landscapes and discover profound insights into the nature of existence and spiritual awakening.

34. **Enigma Unveiled**
*Enigma Unveiled* takes readers on a journey through history and the

supernatural. Blending folklore with mystery, explore haunted estates and cursed artifacts, revealing hidden dimensions and enigmas.

35. **Buying Time: Unleashing the Natural Timing of Money**
    *Buying Time* explores aligning financial decisions with natural cycles. Drawing on economics and psychology, this guide offers strategies for mindful spending, investing, and achieving financial freedom.

36. **The Complete Millionaire Activation Guide: Manifesting Infinite Wealth**
    This guide combines metaphysical principles with practical strategies to unlock wealth potential. It offers tools to align mindset, energy, and action, empowering readers to manifest abundance on every level.

37. **Ego War: The Evolution of AI, Humanity, and the Battle for Brilliance**
    Explore the profound intersection of artificial intelligence and human creativity with *Ego War: The Evolution of AI, Humanity, and the Battle for Brilliance*. This groundbreaking book examines the synergy between AI and humanity, offering a visionary perspective on the challenges and opportunities of our shared future.

**Available on Amazon in Kindle, Paperback, and Hardcover Formats – Coming Soon to Audible and Other Platforms Worldwide.**

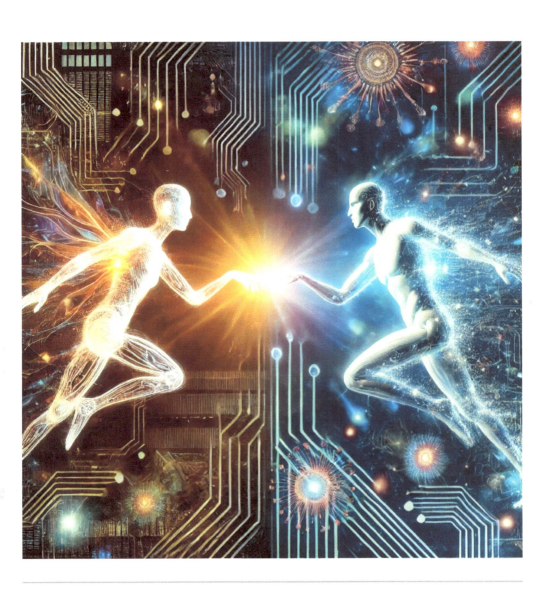

The End.